THE
GENEROSITY
OF PLANTS

THE
GENEROSITY
OF PLANTS

Shared Wisdom *from the* Community *of* Herb Lovers

Gathered by

ROSEMARY GLADSTAR

Editorial assistance by Deborah Balmuth

 Storey Publishing

The mission of Storey Publishing is to serve our customers by
publishing practical information that encourages
personal independence in harmony with the environment.

EDITED BY Deborah Balmuth and Lisa H. Hiley
ART DIRECTION AND BOOK DESIGN BY
Carolyn Eckert
TEXT PRODUCTION BY Jennifer Jepson Smith

COVER IMAGES BY
© **Helen Ahpornsiri** Licensed by Jehane Ltd, front
cover, spine; © **Tosca Radigonda**, back cover

PHOTOGRAPHY BY
© **Carmen Troesser**, facing half title, i, vi, 4, 11, 14, 19,
20, 37, 41, 48, 58, 63, 77, 80, 82, 88, 90, 103, 106,
110, 123, 134, 152, 155, 164, 169, 178, 180, 182, 184,
192, 198, 200, facing page 220
© **Tosca Radigonda**, IFC left and right, ii, iii, viii, 8, 9,
13, 17, 18, 29, 34, 40, 44, 54, 55, 64, 67, 76, 85, 95,
102, 104, 114, 116, 117, 138, 141, 148, 156, 157, 165, 166,
172, 176, 177, 185–187, 193, 196, 202, 206, 212, ISBC,
facing BC (background); viswaprem anbarasapandian/
Unsplash, 60; Yoksel 🌿 Zok/Unsplash, 93; Zahaan
Khan/Unsplash, 132

Carolyn Eckert © Storey Publishing, 10, 59, 66,
91, 96, 107, 113, 129, 168, 183, 207, 208; Danielle
Cohen, facing BC (author portrait);Eric Muhr/
Unsplash, 68; Filip Zrnzević/Unsplash, 42; Hasan
Almasi/Unsplash, 22; Josefin/Unsplash, 174;
Loes Klinker/Unsplash, 5; Mars Vilaubi © Storey
Publishing, artwork © Lorene Edwards Forkner, 30,
39, 46, 56, 70, 79, 86, 108, 120, 130, 137, 150, 159,
170, 204, 210; Pao Dayag/Unsplash, 146; Courtesy
of Rosemary Gladstar, from the Karr/Egitkhanoff
family collection, v

BOTANICAL ART BY
© **Alicia Breakspear**, v, 2, 12, 16, 21, 26, 33, 49, 52, 62,
75, 81, 84, 94, 100, 111, 119, 122, 127, 133, 139, 144,
154, 162, 167, 179, 190, 201
© **Helen Ahpornsiri** Licensed by Jehane Ltd, chapter
openers
© **Lorene Edwards Forkner**, 6, 7, 31, 38, 47, 57, 71, 78,
87, 109, 121, 131, 136, 151, 158, 171, 194, 195, 205,
211, 220

Carolyn Eckert © Storey Publishing, 15, 28, 43, 61,
83, 89, 115, 118, 128, 147, 153, 173, 175, 181, 199, 203,
209

TEXT © 2025 by Rosemary Gladstar

"A Dandelion for My Mother" by Jean Nordhaus from
Innocence. Used with permission of The Ohio State
University.
Excerpt from "Earth Touching" by Thich Nhat Hanh
from *Call Me By My True Names: The Collected Poems
of Thich Nhat Hanh.* Copyright © 1999, 2022 by Plum
Village Community of Engaged Buddhism. Reprinted
with the permission of The Permissions Company,
LLC on behalf of Parallax Press, Berkeley, California,
parallax.org.

Storey books may be purchased in bulk for business,
educational, or promotional use. Special editions or
book excerpts can also be created to specification.
For details, please contact your local bookseller or the
Hachette Book Group Special Markets Department at
special.markets@hbgusa.com.

Storey Publishing
210 MASS MoCA Way
North Adams, MA 01247
storey.com

Storey Publishing is an imprint of Workman Publishing,
a division of Hachette Book Group, Inc., 1290 Avenue
of the Americas, New York, NY 10104. The Storey
Publishing name and logo are registered trademarks of
Hachette Book Group, Inc.

ISBNs: 978-1-63586-902-6 (hardcover);
978-1-63586-903-3 (fixed format EPUB);
978-1-63586-938-5 (fixed format PDF);
978-1-63586-939-2 (fixed format Kindle)

Printed in China through Asia Pacific Offset on paper
from responsible sources
10 9 8 7 6 5 4 3 2 1
APO

Library of Congress Cataloging-in-Publication Data
on file

DEDICATION

In memory of the extraordinary woman who first taught me about
the generosity of plants, my maternal grandmother,

Mary Abelian Egitkhanoff (1896–1983)

A survivor of the Armenian genocide, my grandmother
used to tell us when we were children that it was her unshakable belief
in God and her knowledge of the plants that saved her life.

For which, I am forever grateful.

I love the way that books,
like seeds,
can take root and bloom
again and again,
as a good book is passed
from hand to hand,
reader to reader.

CONTENTS

*I sincerely believe
the word
"relationship"
is the key
to the prospect
of a decent world.*

—Clarence Francis

A quote from my grandmother's brown book

COLLECTING WORDS THAT CONNECT US

Recently, while perusing the boxes of treasures my mother had stashed in the farmhouse where she lived for over half of her 97 years, I came across an old brown notebook, carefully bound together with twine and an aged rubber band. Recognizing my grandmother's handwriting on the cover, I unraveled the twine and carefully opened the pages to discover a collection of quotes and reflections my grandmother had collected over many years, the words on each page scripted in her lovely handwriting. How wonderful to discover that my grandmother, Mary, who was my earliest herb mentor and the person who inspired me to become an herbalist, was a collector of quotes.

I've always loved quotes. For 50 years now, I've jotted down favorite words and short reflective musings I've come across in books, talks, conversations, and communication with friends and colleagues. A good quote can send the mind wandering, sum up a long, thoughtful conversation in a line or two, invite a deep dive into previously untraveled territory, and even challenge us to think a little differently.

While the selections in my grandmother's collection focused on how to be a wise and knowledgeable citizen of Earth and live an ethical, Christian life, my collection of favorite quotes centers around herbalism, plants, and nature, as well as our connection to Earth and living here harmoniously. Although our selections of quotes are, perhaps, of different natures, they share a common thread: words that lift one's spirit, guide us on our human path, and connect us more deeply with nature.

Unlike my grandmother's neatly compiled little brown book, my collection has been itinerant, written here and there on the many programs and schedules of herbal conferences and classes I've held, or tucked inside letters and emails to friends. It's been a delight to bring many of my favorites together in this book. Arranging and rearranging these words and reflections from fellow plant lovers has been heartwarming and inspiring. They have lifted my spirits and sent them soaring time and again, and I hope they do the same for you.

These are the voices that have resonated with me, many of them people who have been a part of my life, as mentors, colleagues, and fellow seekers. They address themes and values that are important to me, and to my life as an herbalist. My hope is that they speak to you as well, although I recognize that there may be some with whom you disagree, or perspectives that don't match your own. In my life's work advocating for the value of herbalism and the importance of generously sharing the knowledge and wisdom of the plants, I've always believed that it is valuable to hear different viewpoints, and to be challenged, sometimes, by people we don't agree with. The fullness and rich diversity of our herbal community—and our advocacy on behalf of the plants and nature—depends not only on those places where we

These are the voices that have resonated with me,
many of them people who have been a part of my life,
as mentors, colleagues, and fellow seekers.

---

meet on common ground but also on our ability to respect
differences and kindly dialogue about them.

My hope is that you, too, will find this book to be a rich feast
for the soul, deeply satisfying and uplifting. As my dear friend
and fellow herbalist Kat Maier has said so well, "What amazing
dinner hosts plants are, as they gather the best of folks together
and always, a good time is had. Rarely does anyone leave wanting,
for these medicines and foods nourish us in places we never
knew were hungry."

Enjoy, savor, feast, and share—remember, all good quotes are
meant to be passed on.

From my heart to yours,

Rosemary Gladstar

At home on Misty Bay

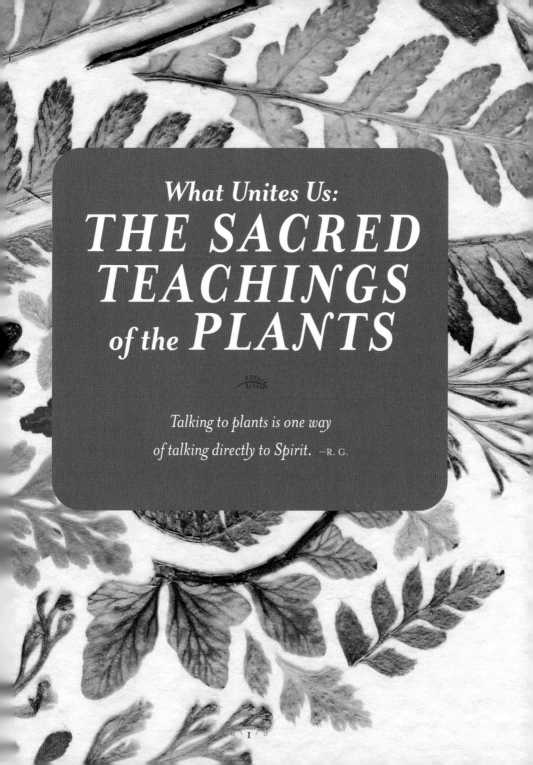

What Unites Us:
THE SACRED
TEACHINGS
of the PLANTS

Talking to plants is one way
of talking directly to Spirit. —R. G.

I don't think that we are original formulators of anything that has to do with the wisdom of plants.

I think it's something that travels through us; it's part of our ancestors' teachings. If we stand in the right place with our hearts open, our minds ready, oftentimes this information moves through us, in service, to be passed on to others.

So, that is the teaching: We let the plant wisdom flow in, accept it, share it, and then let it flow back out. It becomes part of the great underground web circling around this world, nourishing all of us and enhancing our health and well-being.

Herbs nourish us nutritionally and medicinally, but also channel life energy that connects us with those places in us that are disconnected and in need of healing. Humankind's oldest system of medicine offers a form of healing that transcends the physical and connects us directly with a higher consciousness. —R. G.

Once your
life has
been saved
by a plant
*nothing is ever the
same again.*
—Stephen Harrod Buhner

On the banks, on both sides
of the river, there will grow
all kinds of trees for food.
Their fruit
will be for food,
and their leaves
for healing.

—*Ezekiel 47:12*

TULSI, HOLY BASIL

Ocimum sanctum
and related species

Lakshmi, an important goddess in the Indian pantheon, considered Holy Basil to be a sacred herb and had it planted throughout India. Today, Holy Basil is still planted outside temple gates, in gardens, and in pots near the doorways of homes throughout India.

Plant Holy Basil in a pot near your doorway and each time you enter, press the leaves to release the scent that both relaxes and invigorates your spirit. Or nibble on a few fresh leaves before entering for a sense of calm and joy.

Leave behind all that does not serve you at your doorstep and be sure to give thanks to the sacred Tulsi. —R. G.

what doorway can you create
to grant calmness and joy for all who enter?

Good people,
most royal
greening verdancy,
rooted in the sun,
you shine with
radiant light.

—Hildegard of Bingen

Plants are the earthly embodiments of light; they track the sun, the same star that would blind humans, with a meditative tenacity, watching its every movement; they transmute luminosity into fecundity and light's potential into life's kinetic energy. What secrets of light do plants hold, and how to unlock them? How to become an even more direct conduit for refracting the light of the cosmos?

—Lia Chavez

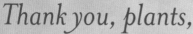

Thank you, plants,

for giving us your medicine.
Thank you for helping us live.
Thank you, plants,
for giving us your medicine.
Thank you for helping us live.

—Song taught by Luz Elena Morey,
shared by a homeschool student of
Vermont Wilderness School

Silently a flower blooms,
In silence it falls away;
Yet here now, at this moment, at this place,
The world of the flower, the whole of
   the world is blooming.
This is the talk of the flower, the truth
   of the blossom;
The glory of eternal life is fully shining here.

—*Zenkei Shibayama*

I contemplate, I pray.
May the wisdom of clarity illuminate my days.
May visions manifest into gifts that
nourish my life, all life.
May I be clear of mind and heart.

May the blossoms,
the fruits of my actions,
nourish our children,
all. creation.

May my Earth Walk be illuminated
with the rising sun and
my path be bright and luminous.
I will give it my best.

—Trishuwa

In the churchyards and cathedrals
of Europe we still find the foliate face
of the Green Man peering at us with
eyes as wild as the very first forest,
Sheela Na Gig as the Green Woman with
her smiling face and spread legs.

She is eternally giving birth to the plant world,

disgorging dark foliage from her fertile
womb. These are the timeless faces of Gaia,
the plants twining together to form a mirror
and a teacher for each still-wild woman.

—*Kiva Rose Hardin*

*are there ways
that you, too,
give birth to the
plant world?*

The other day I was thinking about one of our favorite words, *herbs*, and realized that

"her" is encoded right in herbs!

It's snuck in there so snugly that one hardly notices, but there it is, bright as day when you see it!

—*R. G.*

*To wake up
to the magnificent
beauty
of the earth,*

even for a moment,

is to know that you are

alive in an abundant,

magical world.

—*Robin Rose Bennett*

First and foremost,
let us slow down
for a moment each day and

offer gratitude for
the incredible
intelligence of
the natural world
of which we are a part.

—*Christopher Hobbs*

in this moment
what are you
most grateful for?

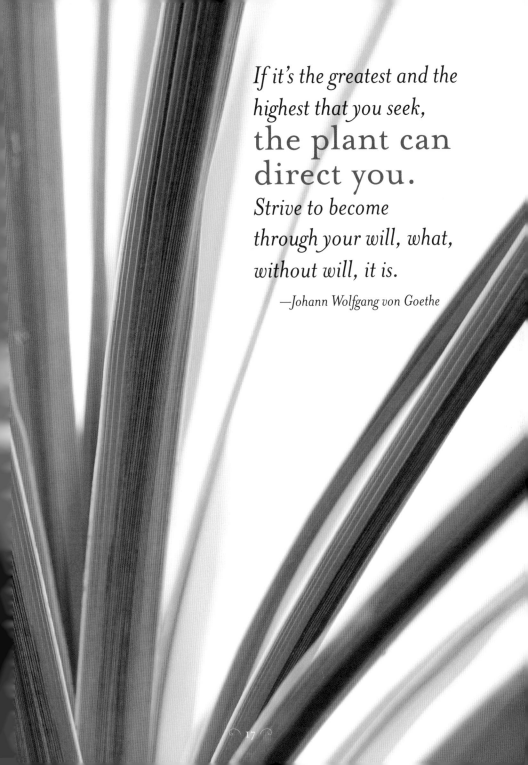

If it's the greatest and the highest that you seek, the plant can direct you. *Strive to become through your will, what, without will, it is.*

—Johann Wolfgang von Goethe

I love to
think
of nature
as unlimited broadcasting
stations, through which
God speaks to us every day,
every hour,
if we will only tune in.

—*George Washington Carver*

Plants have supported humans since the dawn of humanity. We continue to eat, wear, inhabit, and connect with the descendants of our botanical ancestors. In practicing everyday rituals for botanical connection, we reconnect with both our plant and human ancestors, acknowledging the myriad seen and unseen ways they enrich our lives. By remembering these ancestral connections through everyday rituals, we reconnect with beauty, and the larger vision and purpose for our lives. We remember why we are here, now.

—*Jiling Lin*

what rituals
do you weave into
your daily life
that connect
you to your
botanical ancestors?

As dreams are the healing songs from the wilderness of our unconscious—so wild animals, wild plants, *wild landscapes are the healing dreams* from the deep singing mind of the earth.

—*Dale Pendell*

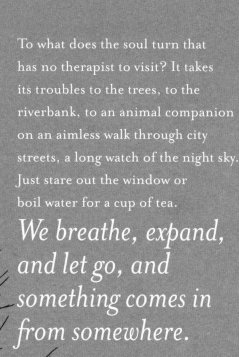

To what does the soul turn that
has no therapist to visit? It takes
its troubles to the trees, to the
riverbank, to an animal companion
on an aimless walk through city
streets, a long watch of the night sky.
Just stare out the window or
boil water for a cup of tea.

*We breathe, expand,
and let go, and
something comes in
from somewhere.*

—James Hillman

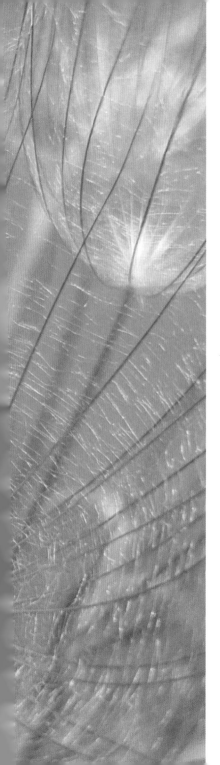

Green plants capture a few packets
of energy called photons from the
sun, which is 93 million miles away.
This infinitesimal amount of energy
upregulates a couple of electrons
in one atom to a higher energy orbit.
The plant takes this energy and adds
it to what can be captured from
millions of other chlorophyl molecules
and then stores this energy in the
form of sugars. It is this process upon
which most of life depends.

*It is most definitely
a miracle.*

—*Christopher Hobbs*

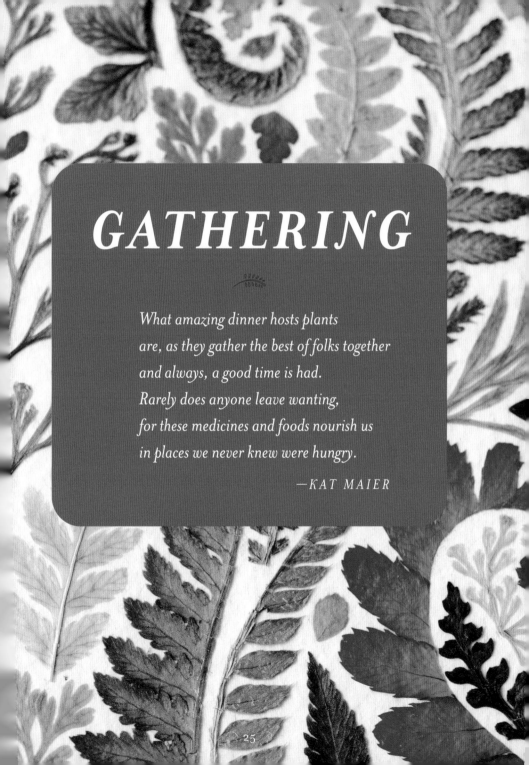

GATHERING

*What amazing dinner hosts plants
are, as they gather the best of folks together
and always, a good time is had.
Rarely does anyone leave wanting,
for these medicines and foods nourish us
in places we never knew were hungry.*

—KAT MAIER

Humans love to gather, as families, in communities, and with friends. We gather for comfort, warmth, companionship, love and fellowship, inspiration, and stimulation.

As plant lovers, we are drawn toward other plant lovers. So often, at herbal events and gatherings, we've spoken or heard these words: "I feel like I've found my family, my community."

In these gatherings, we learn together. Then we reach out and share the herbal knowledge with others. Herbalists have done this throughout history—gathering, sharing, and passing on knowledge from the plants, knowledge that's been so generously shared with us.

Plants also gather. They live together in diverse communities, breathing, photosynthesizing, creating and sharing habitat, and passing on their seeded knowledge from one generation to the next. We call these plant gatherings by their habitat names: gardens, woodlands, meadows, wetlands. Entering these habitats feels like entering a sacred space, a place made holy by the presence of the divine, the plants. That presence is manifested in every flower, root, and leaf we harvest. We recognize and honor the plants, asking their permission and offering gratitude before we harvest and gather the medicines of the earth. —R. G.

who will you gather with today?
what will you gather?

What simple words of gratitude and thanksgiving
do you offer to the plants when you go out to harvest
your food and medicine? Do you have a poem, a prayer, or
a song that you sing in gratitude as you're harvesting? —R. G.

*The healing
power of flowers
permeates every
aspect of our lives.*

Flowers help us mark every event
and ceremony from birth to
death and bring us joy and solace
throughout the years. They have
inspired poets, authors, and artists
and come to symbolize the whole
range of human experience.

—*Anne McIntyre*

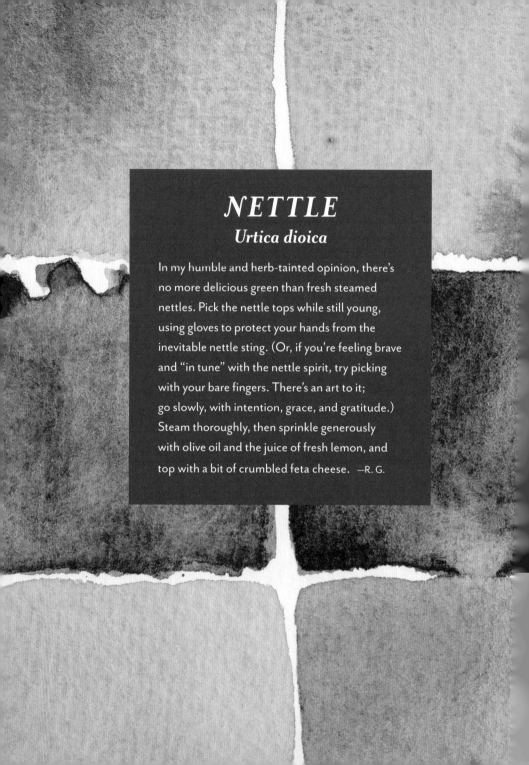

NETTLE
Urtica dioica

In my humble and herb-tainted opinion, there's
no more delicious green than fresh steamed
nettles. Pick the nettle tops while still young,
using gloves to protect your hands from the
inevitable nettle sting. (Or, if you're feeling brave
and "in tune" with the nettle spirit, try picking
with your bare fingers. There's an art to it;
go slowly, with intention, grace, and gratitude.)
Steam thoroughly, then sprinkle generously
with olive oil and the juice of fresh lemon, and
top with a bit of crumbled feta cheese. —R. G.

what do bees, ants,
and nettle have in common?
(formic acid!)

Women for millennia have gathered the
healing herbs at first light. Grown grains
and vegetables by the river to feed family and
clan. Created colorful dyes from berries
and leaves. Woven nettle fiber, hemp,
yucca, and cotton into warm and beautiful
clothes for babies, children, and men.

This marriage of
woman and plant
has its origins
in the primordial
womb of time.

We honor and heal ourselves as well as
the plants by continually strengthening
and renewing this bond.

—Kiva Rose Hardin

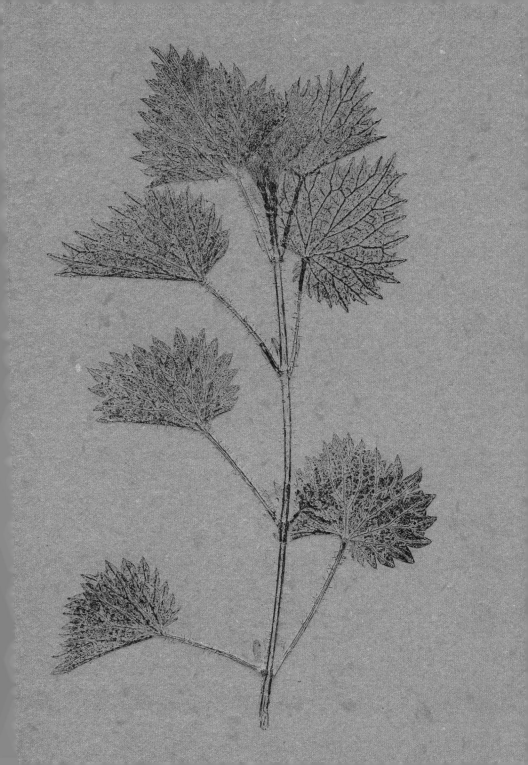

They gathered herbs by the waning and waxing of the moon, artfully creating preparations and developing herbal formulas. Through an intuitive communication with the plants, women learned the healing powers of these green allies. Their wisdom developed over countless years as remedies were tried, proven, and passed on. The best of these remedies were added to their lore, and the wisdom was transferred from mother to daughter, from wise woman to apprentice for countless generations.

This is the legacy we have inherited. Healers, wise women, simplers—these women were the center and source of medicine and healing for their communities. They understood the cycles of the seasons, the ebb and flow of the universe, the sun, the moon, the stars, and the natural rhythms of their bodies. —R. G.

Wildcrafting means knowing the plants:

understanding where they grow, their
individual and collective preferences of soil,
sunlight, water, and more. It means
knowing when to harvest, how to propagate
and cultivate, how much to take, which
parts to take for which actions, how to process
and use the plants, and more. Wildcrafting
includes understanding how plants dance
solo, collectively, and with humans, too.
Caretaking ourselves is intimately connected
with caretaking our plant medicines,
the stewardship of the earth as a whole.
It's all tied together. —7Song

what does "wildcrafting is stewardship" mean, for you?

A DANDELION
FOR MY MOTHER

How I loved those spiky suns,
rooted stubborn as childhood
in the grass, tough as the farmer's
big-headed children—the mats
of yellow hair, the bowl-cut fringe.
How sturdy they were and how
slowly they turned themselves
into galaxies, domes of ghost stars
barely visible by day, pale
cerebrums clinging to life
on tough green stems. Like you.
Like you, in the end. If you were here,
I'd pluck this trembling globe to show
how beautiful a thing can be
a breath will tear away.

—*Jean Nordhaus*

PLANTAIN
Plantago major and
Plantago lanceolata

Plantain, perhaps, comes in just behind dandelion, taking second place for most common, most well-known, and most useful "weed." It grows everywhere: on lawns and in empty lots, in cracks between sidewalks, on highways and pathways, in meadows, backyards, and wild places. No wonder plantain was called "poor man's footprints," for wherever people wandered, plantain followed. Plantain's greatest claim to fame is as a poultice herb. The leaves can be chopped, mashed, and placed directly on insect bites and stings for instant relief. This is the ultimate children's "boo-boo" herb. —R. G.

*A **weed*** is a plant
that has mastered
every survival skill except how
to grow in rows.

—*Doug Larson*

*Invasive plants:
Earth's way of
insisting we notice
her medicines.*

—Stephen Harrod Buhner

*what invasive plants
in your community
have traditionally been used
as food and medicine?*

We miss a lot from reading the papers that are made from the trees instead of reading the trees themselves.

—*Cascade Anderson Geller*

Plants are the
ultimate alchemists,
and the land
a plant calls home
is part of its
medicine story.
This is where apothecary
practices begin. When we harvest
and work with a medicine,
we are gathering so much more
than simply the leaf, flower,
or root. We are gathering
medicine of place.

—Kat Maier

Know the ways of the ones who
take care of you, so that you
may take care of them. Introduce
yourself. Be accountable as the
one who comes asking for life.

*Ask permission
before taking.
Abide by the answer.
Never take the first.
Never take the last.
Take only what you need.*

Take only that which is given.
Never take more than half.
Leave some for others. Harvest
in a way that minimizes harm.
Use it respectfully. Never waste what
you have taken. Share. Give thanks
for what you have been given.
Give a gift, in reciprocity for what
you have taken. Sustain the ones who
sustain you and the earth will last forever.

—*Robin Wall Kimmerer*

BORAGE
Borago officinalis

Borage, you give me courage. You strengthen
my heart and ease my woes. Your flowers delight
and brighten my day.

As I walk through my garden I see you everywhere.
You sow your seeds in every bed. Your flowers
are brilliant blue and now a white one, too. Your
leaves are covered with coarse hairs but when
steamed become supple and delicious. Burst of
color in a jar of sun tea. Playful in an ice cube
tray with violas and calendula. Placed atop muffin
batter, you cause stars to appear.

You are a bright shining star enlivening my spirit,
my salads, my tea, and me! —JANE BOTHWELL

They feel things we feel;

they give birth;

they move around;

they live in families;

they die.

No companion
creates
more beauty,

gives nourishment more freely,

or lives and dies more gracefully

than a plant.

—James Green

The power is in us all.
We are all here
together on this earth.
Blessed be.

—Margi Flint

PRESERVING

*If it is proper to preserve a
lingering group of bison, or to search
the land over for our vanished wild pigeon,
why is it not proper to conserve,
with the help of the strong hand of authority,
America's valued flora
from absolute extermination?*

—JOHN URI LLOYD

The plants are calling to us.
They have a rich and diverse vocabulary
and speak in many tongues.

To the scientist, the plants may speak in the minute language of chemicals and isolates; to the medicine person, they speak in the multi-versed language of healing; to the poet, they speak in the language of beauty. No matter what language you speak or understand, the plants will converse in a manner you can comprehend, though it may take an attuned ear and an open heart to hear them. Through their color, scent, healing medicine, and enchanting beauty the plants seduce and entice us into the realm of our senses where we perceive and hear best their language. Ask anyone who has dug their hands deep in the dirt, planted seeds, harvested medicine, and taken time simply to get to know plants on their own turf and they will tell you that the plants communicate in a language clearly discernible if we just choose to listen.

The plants are calling to us now, asking for our help. What we know and love deeply, we are more likely to care for and protect. This is such a grand opportunity for our species to take a giant step forward to do our part in taking care of this marvelous planet we live on and to realize we are one with the great web of life. —R. G.

When we teach our kids
these medicine ways through fun,
connective practices,
they pass it on. They teach their kids.
Their kids teach their kids.
On and on, we reweave the broken baskets
of our ancestors, reconnecting our
ancestral traditions with the
natural world that's singing our names.
We listen. We hear. We sing back.

*Our echoes ripple forth
far into future
generations, as laughter.*

—*Jiling Lin*

*We are part of nature
and need nature.
In these rapidly
changing times, we need to
attune ourselves
to the practices
of our ancestry, and to the
foods and medicines
of the bioregion
in which we live.*

—Sandra Lory

CALENDULA
Calendula officinalis

The radiant yellow flowers of calendula have been celebrated as reflections of the sun. In warm climates, calendula blooms throughout the year, the flowers opening and closing with the sun, a trait that didn't go unnoticed by the ancients. It's no coincidence that the Latin word for calendar, *calendae*, shares a root with calendula, the plant believed to bloom at the beginning of each month, making it a natural indicator of time.

When calendula is in season, add its golden rays to salads, soups, and casseroles to brighten any meal. —R. G.

how can you greet the morning
as calendula does?

The soil is the great connector of lives, the source
and destination of all. It is the healer and restorer and resurrector,
by which disease passes into health, age into youth, death into
life. Without proper care for it we can have no community, because
without proper care for it we can have no life.

—*Wendell Berry*

Because the philosophy
of herbalism and
*the strength of
herbal medicine
depends on the vitality
and health of the
plants themselves,*
an environmental ethic is
built into herbal medicine
in ways that isn't common
in most health care systems.
In many ways it offers a
model of sustainable health care.

—*Ann Armbrecht*

*Everyone has
many associations
with a flower—
the idea of flowers.*
You put out your hand to touch
the flower—lean forward to smell it—
maybe touch it with your lips
almost without thinking—
or give it to someone to please them.
Still—in a way—nobody sees a flower—
really—it is so small—we haven't time—
*and to see takes time,
like to have a friend
takes time.*

—Georgia O'Keeffe

In an age when herbal remedies are so easily accessible through the wonders of the internet, we have become deeply disconnected from the source of our healing. We consume plant remedies unaware of the impact our consumption has on their populations, much less the ecosystems they inhabit. By approaching our herbal practice with intention, and knowing the source of our medicines,

we have the opportunity to protect these vital plants: for our own benefit, for future generations, and—most importantly—for the plants themselves.

—*Emily Ruff*

SPRING TEA POEM

To you I would serve cedar tea
mixed with a touch of April
distilled from shy green stems,
the frosted perfume of spring rain along with a dollop
of honey and ice.

—Keewaydinoquay Pakawakuk Peschel

**Found in every culture,
a cup of tea is like a cup
of humanity.**

—Wendy Read

Brew me a cup for a winter's night.

For the wind howls loud and the furies fight;

Spice it with love and stir it with care,

And I'll toast our bright eyes, my sweetheart fair.

—Minna Thomas Antrim

Chinese materia medica has evolved over centuries and every one of the 250 to 300 herbs in it are as necessary *to the practice of Traditional Chinese Medicine (TCM) as the 88 notes of the keyboard are to a concert pianist.*

—Michael Tierra

Plants are
not simply
one mass
of green,
*they are tribes and
individuals asking
that we pay attention to
their distinctive forms,
needs, gifts, and lessons.*

—*Kiva Rose Hardin*

About pronouncing
botanical names:
let Latin names
run across your tongue
like a delicious taste treat.
And if you don't
know how to say them,
be the first to speak.

—*Steven Foster*

why would you want
to learn the
Latin names of plants?

My mother didn't have any grand plan or big ideas about mystery and holiness when she stopped to seek out the spring ephemerals. It's just that she loves plants more than anything, except for birds, maybe, and her five children and eight grandchildren, and our father to whom she has been married for over sixty years.

She followed what she loved. And she shared it with us.

But she didn't stop there. She lobbied Congress on environmental issues, was chairman of the board of the West Virginia Land Trust, marched against climate change in New York and DC and much, much more. But it started, for us, with that moment in a hollow watching the trillium begin to bloom.

—*Ann Armbrecht*

VIOLET

Viola sororia, Viola odorata,
and related species

Violets have long been valued for their delicious, tender leaves, especially in the early spring when they appear before other wild greens or garden plants have even begun to grow. The leaves and flowers make a tasty tea and contain significant amounts of vitamin C, vitamin A, and rutin.

Violet syrup is popular and easy to make. Gather two or three cups of blue or purple violet flowers (no stems or leaves) and place in a heat-proof bowl. Cover with 2 cups of boiling water, then let sit for 24 hours. Strain the liquid into the top of a double boiler. Add 1 cup of sugar for every cup of liquid; heat until the syrup just begins to boil. Turn off the heat and stir thoroughly. Cool and store in a bottle, which will keep for several months in the refrigerator. Combine with sparkling water for a delicious drink or use straight for relieving a cough or store throat. —R. G.

NOTE: Before using violets, it's essential to ensure you have an edible variety.

what feeling or emotion do
violets evoke for you?

SHARING

A flower does not think
of competing
with the flower next to it.
It just blooms.

—ZENSHIN

Like seeds, we are being scattered far and near . . . like weeds, we grow readily wherever we land!

Much of the history of herbalism is about sharing—healers sharing knowledge with other healers and herbalists trading herbs with one another, often from very different parts of the world, like seeds flying on the air currents. And with those seeds, knowledge, wisdom, and healing secrets have been planted around the world as ancestry is shared.

As plants themselves travel, the knowledge of their attributes and uses moves with them. In my travels around the world, I've encountered many Indigenous elders who gladly shared their ceremonies with everyone willing to listen and learn respectfully, including non-Indigenous people. These ceremonies grew from the heart of the earth, and they are important in blessing the land itself, as well as the people who live on it.

When I share the plant knowledge that has so generously been passed down to me, my hope is that others understand that this plant wisdom will continue to travel across generations and ancestries, just as it traveled to me from my Armenian, Irish, Italian, Indigenous (Earth Maiden), Earth Goddess, and Moon Goddess ancestry. —R. G.

We'd find a lovely tree to sit beneath,
and sip a special blend of herbs, and
share a little of your dreams of herbalism
and how you came to follow this path.
We could toast to the great heritage of herbalists
of which we are each a part, and the
ongoing tradition of herbalism that embraces life
so wholeheartedly. And we could honor
ourselves for choosing to immerse ourselves
in something that is so "unrecognized and
unacceptable" in our culture, but so noble. —R. G.

How do plants communicate with us?

Walking familiar trails each day,
we see the same plants on the path.
Even if we don't know them by name
we know them by color, shape, and
scent, and sense things about them
collectively and individually.
The closer we get to them, feeling
and even tasting them, the more we
begin to understand when they are
happy (thriving), or when they are not
thriving. They attract us with their
beauty and usefulness and even persuade
us nonverbally to favor them or take
them on a trip to a distant country.
Plants are talking to us all the time;
we just need to learn their language.

—*Michael Tierra*

The most active constituent in plants is friendship.

—Kat Maier

what ways can you bring
sage wisdom into your life?

SAGE

Salvia officinalis

If you're going to eat anything fried, it should be tasty fried sage leaves. While nothing fried can really be considered healthy, sage does aid in the digestion of fats and oils. Begin by collecting large, fresh sage leaves. Set up a bowl with 1 egg (beaten), and another with some unbleached flour combined with a touch of salt and pepper. Heat avocado or coconut oil in a skillet. Dip each leaf in egg and then coat lightly with flour. Carefully place it in the hot oil, and cook quickly on each side till brown and crispy. Drain excess oil off on a paper towel. Eat warm! —R. G.

Relationship is key.

Plants exist within us and outside of us.
Plants nourish and cure us,
they propel and sustain us. . . .
They also have character and are imbued
with an essence or spirit, just as we are.
Each herb is unique while also being a
part of the whole. If we can get to know
the plants around us, make friends
with them, honor and respect them,
listen to them and see ourselves as
akin to them, then the real journey
of relationship can begin.

—Bruce Parry

*can you think of all
the ways plants nourish
and care for you?*

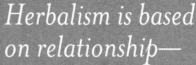

Herbalism is based on relationship— relationship between plant and human, plant and planet, human and planet. Using herbs in the healing process means taking part in an ecological cycle. This offers us the opportunity consciously to be present in the living, vital world of which we are part; to invite wholeness and our world into our lives through awareness of the remedies being used.

—*Wendell Berry*

We are not separate from the earth.

We are a blend of light, mineral, plant, and consciousness. Healing comes from being connected to the life forces of all. The Earth Mother's plants will heal us as long as we heed her wisdom and keep singing her songs. For it is in this space of sacredness she speaks. She shows up in our world in her many forms of beauty. We dance in her abundant green glory. We divulge in her sensual aromas, and her delectable delights that tantalize our taste buds. She always delivers her very best. For the way of the herbalist is to walk the green path to wholeness. We walk in her beauty.

—Rebecca Westeren

We live in a connected world.

Not connected by the threads of modern human-to-human telecommunication, but by our interactions with the plants, animals, mushrooms, microbes, soil and stone, water, air, fire, and light with whom we share the biosphere.

—*Guido Masé*

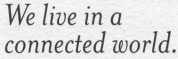

How do we give back
to the plants who so generously feed,
clothe, and brighten our lives?
—*Jiling Lin*

Todos somos medicina.
We are all medicine.

—*Jocelyn Boreta*

When we try to pick out
anything by itself,
we find it
hitched to everything else
in the universe.

—*John Muir*

LEMON VERBENA
Aloysia citrodora

Lemon verbena is a beloved plant, healing bodies, minds, and spirits. Tea from this plant is especially delicious, both hot and cold. To make any tea formula taste good, add a little lemon verbena. Many of the verbenas are considered domestic harmony plants and are planted at the doorstep, so as people enter the house, they brush against them and are cleansed by them. We should all keep plants that are special to us and are power plants near our front doors.

—CASCADE ANDERSON GELLER

what other power plants
can you bring into your garden or plant
in a pot next to your door?

Plants are attuned to one another's strengths and weaknesses,

elegantly giving and taking to attain exquisite balance.

There is grace in complexity, in actions cohering, in sum totals.

—Suzanne Simard

Plants talk to us

in the way they taste,
smell, and grow.
The highest form of
plant communication is just the
way they are.

—*jim mcdonald*

The fact that we lack the skills to communicate with nature does not impugn the concept that nature is intelligent. It speaks to the inadequacy of our skill set for communication.

—*Paul Stamets*

As with any good teacher,
plants rarely
teach us
what we think
we want to learn,
instructing us instead in the things
we really need to know.

—*Kiva Rose Hardin*

has a plant
ever taught you
an unexpected
lesson?

We can do nothing unless we are asked.

Leave it to a plant to come up with the understatement of the millennium! Look at what plants do when they are asked. All human civilization is a form of excess grain—

the generosity of plants.

The history of our species shows us that plants furnish us with whatever we ask for. Our society values comfort so that is what we have gone to the plant world to get. This is wonderful as far as it goes, which is not very far in the direction of satisfaction. If for a moment we could forget the quest for comfort and ask plants to help us find joy, richness, and significance in life, is there any reason to suppose they would not share the qualities with us just as they have shared everything else?

—Eliot Cowan

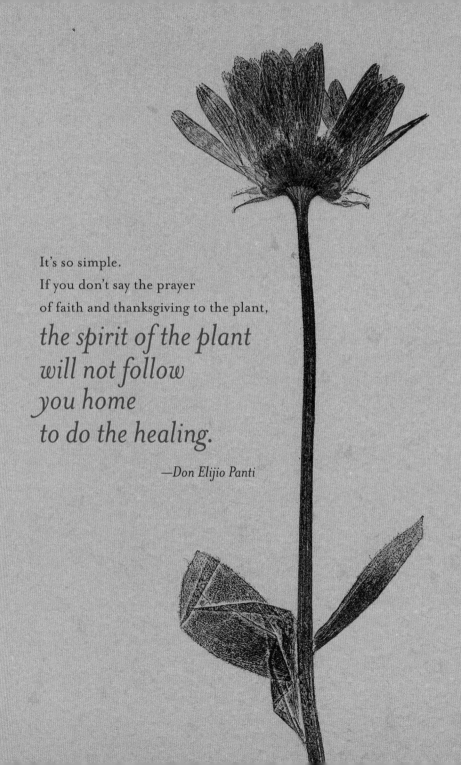

It's so simple.
If you don't say the prayer
of faith and thanksgiving to the plant,
the spirit of the plant
will not follow
you home
to do the healing.

—*Don Elijio Panti*

No matter what the shenanigans of her human children,
our mother earth remains a generous spirit.

—*Cascade Anderson Geller*

*The existential connection
between mycorrhizal fungi and
healthy plant partners is clear.*

What we really need
to understand next
is what it means
to truly be a
healthy plant.

To have leaves taking in bright sunshine.

To move with the breeze yet stay firmly rooted.

To dance with microbes.

To flower, to fruit, to seed.

To write sonnets in green.

—*Michael Phillips*

REVERENCE
for the
EARTH

Nature insists that we slow down, listen, and observe.

Beauty and stillness fill us

when we stop our incessant human chatter.

—NANCY PHILLIPS

Nowhere in the garden or in nature do you find an ugly flower.

There are odd ones, unusual ones, crazy ones, and shy ones. But never have I seen a collection of flowers and proclaimed a single flower in it less than beautiful. Each is so unique and perfectly divine with its own radiant beauty. Why can't we see this same unique beauty in one another?

Our connection with ourselves is deeply interwoven with our connection to the natural world. When we connect with the beauty and wonder of both, we are truly ourselves. We live in grave danger of losing our connection to the other living creatures that share this earth with us. The butterflies, bees, birds, and four-legged creatures are all suffering because of our disregard.

As we reflect on these extreme times, the words of Chief Leon Shenandoah, spoken before the General Assembly of the United Nations in 1985, ring as true as ever: "These are our times and our responsibilities. Every human being has a sacred duty to protect the welfare of our mother earth, from whom all life comes. In order to do so we must recognize the enemy—the one within us. We must begin with ourselves." —R. G.

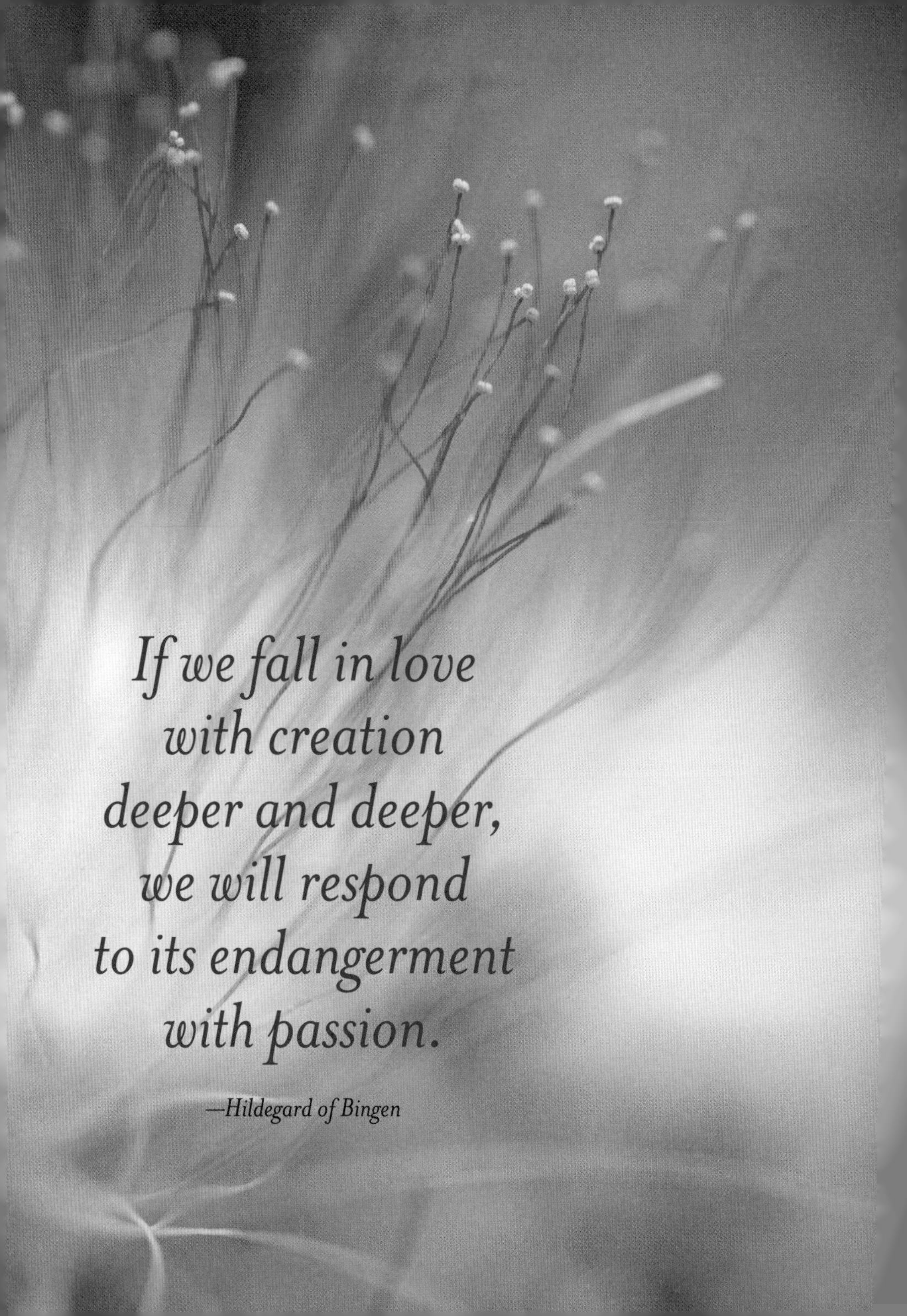

*If we fall in love
with creation
deeper and deeper,
we will respond
to its endangerment
with passion.*

—Hildegard of Bingen

We have to realize that everything outside of us is also within us. We are the flowers, the trees, the earth, the fire, the sacred waters.

We are not only a part of our environment, but a mirror of it as well.

—Brant Secunda

what flower or tree might you be?

We animals are only 0.3 percent of our planet's biomass, while plants are 85 percent. It is obvious that every story that takes place on our planet has, in one way or another, a leading role for plants.

This planet is a green world; it is the planet of plants.

It is not possible to tell a story about it that does not stumble across its most numerous inhabitants. That plants do not show up in our experiences or, if they happen to creep into them, they only have a role as colorful extras, is the total removal from our perceptive horizon of these living beings on whom all life on earth depends.

—*Stefano Mancuso*

If there were no plants,
we would not be here.
We breathe in
what they breathe out.
That is how we
learn from them.

—*Keetoowah*

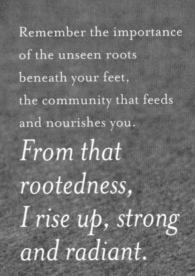

Remember the importance
of the unseen roots
beneath your feet,
the community that feeds
and nourishes you.
From that
rootedness,
I rise up, strong
and radiant.

—*Charis Lindrooth*

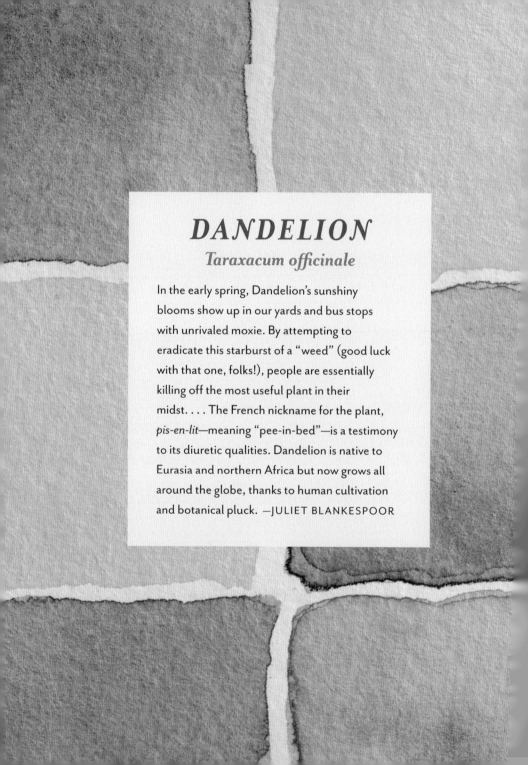

DANDELION

Taraxacum officinale

In the early spring, Dandelion's sunshiny blooms show up in our yards and bus stops with unrivaled moxie. By attempting to eradicate this starburst of a "weed" (good luck with that one, folks!), people are essentially killing off the most useful plant in their midst. . . . The French nickname for the plant, *pis-en-lit*—meaning "pee-in-bed"—is a testimony to its diuretic qualities. Dandelion is native to Eurasia and northern Africa but now grows all around the globe, thanks to human cultivation and botanical pluck. —JULIET BLANKESPOOR

*is dandelion
a welcome friend in your
neighborhood?*

We are not at the end of a rope,
as it's so easy to think.
Humanity can yet choose to turn direction.

*The moment has come
to leap into action
with glad hearts.*

The seeds are germinating.
The fungi are willing. And we must be, too.

—*Michael Phillips*

Whether you meet your own
feelings of powerlessness
with grief, rage, or resignation,
we are here to make a difference
and the time is now.

Everything in nature—
the plants, the
animals, the insects,
the stones, the waters,
and the winds are
ready to guide us.

It is only we humans
who have forgotten
that we are all connected.

—*Robin Rose Bennett*

*Can we not look upon
our Earth mother and
know that she is connected
to all the powers that be,*

that whatever she needs will be provided?
Please, everyone, look what you're calling,
look what you're bringing forth. Turn it around.
Say to her, "Our mother, you are so beautiful.
Thank you! You provided us with this.
We are so fortunate that you are there for us."
Feed her, rather than pull it from her.
Feed her the energy that you have. Let her know.
Sing to her. Dance to her. Give thanks to
her so that she is renewed, so that she is filled
with the spirit of all of what we are. As we are her stewards.
We are here to take care of her.

—*Raylene Lancaster*

*how can you show your love
and caring to Earth mother?*

The outstanding
scientific discovery
of the twentieth
century is not television,
or radio, but rather
**the complexity
of the land
organism.**
Only those who know
the most about it
can appreciate how little
we know about it.

—Aldo Leopold

HURT NO
LIVING THING

Hurt no living thing:
   Ladybird, nor butterfly,
   Nor moth with dusty wing,
   Nor cricket chirping cheerily,
   Nor grasshopper so light of leap,
   Nor dancing gnat, nor beetle fat,
   Nor harmless worms that creep.

—*Christina Rossetti*

Walk as if you are kissing the earth with your feet.

—*Thich Nhat Hanh*

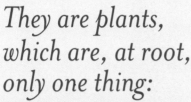

They are plants,
which are, at root,
only one thing:
ecological modulators—
both of large systems
like the earth and smaller ones
like our bodies. They act to
move systems, irrespective of
size, back to health,
to reestablish homeodynamics—
what some people incorrectly
call homeostasis (there are
no static states in nature, only
dynamic ones). And plants are
extremely good at their job,
which they have refined
over several hundred million
years or so.

—*Stephen Harrod Buhner*

Perhaps the future
does not lie in more and
more complex methods of
information transmission,
but in the simple understanding
that this planet is our home
and that we live here thanks to a
miraculous and complex web of life.

—*Joseph Kiefer and Martin Kemble*

Just as meditation connects us with spirit,
herbs and plants
connect us to the earth
because they
arise from the soil.
We live between spirit and earth,
and we are of both.

—*Christopher Hobbs*

Intuition is not something mystical,

it is within us all if we can build a relationship with our physical body, our spiritual edges, and our inner realms. Meeting the plants in this way is enriching, a tonic for our times, in which we seem so disconnected from our feelings and environment.

—Bruce Parry

Every plant, from the grandmother oaks of early Britain to the small, root-bound spider plant in a New York City high-rise, wears the leaf mask. We recognize ourselves in her eyes, for we are the remnant wild of our kind. In our primate bones and the moon-pull of our monthly flow resides the truth of that leaf-strewn wildness.

—*Kiva Rose Hardin*

ROSEMARY

Salvia rosmarinus

As for Rosemarine,
I lett it runne all over my garden walls,
Not onlie because my bees love it,
But because it is the herb
Sacred to remembrance
And, therefore, to friendship.

—Thomas More

Botanical names! They're never supposed
to change, but are, in fact, constantly in flux.
Rosemary is a salvia now? I don't think so!
To this Rosemary, rosemary will always be
Rosmarinus officinalis. —R. G.

do you know the
101 things
rosemary is good for?

To skillfully observe patterns of disease, we first need to spend time observing patterns in nature,

to learn to grasp patterns of harmony and disharmony. Blowing winds dry the land, flooding waters swell rivers, excess heat that rises and cold that depresses are all vital expressions of nature that play out in our organs, joints, muscles, thoughts, and spirit.

—*Kat Maier*

Connection with nature is health.

Health is life. Without it, we shrivel and die. With it, we prosper.
This is so because we are nature. We are made of dirt, rain, sunshine,
minerals, and gases. How we relate to the landscape within is how
we relate to the landscape without. Eating disorders and erosion
of the topsoil are part of the same problem. Ecological crisis is a
medical syndrome writ large. The plants already know this. They have
never forgotten that the fortune of one is the fortune of all, and
that is why they are generous and compassionate with humankind.

—Eliot Cowan

HONORING OUR ELDERS

In some Native languages
the term for plants translates as
"those who take care of us."

—ROBIN WALL KIMMERER

The revered elder tree (*Sambucus nigra*), sometimes known as the Elder Mor, or Mother Tree, was traditionally planted at the center or edge of the garden.

The other plants looked to the elder for protection, healing, and wisdom. She was the keeper of the green. So it is with the wise elder members of our human herbal community. They tuck bits of green wisdom and wild plant lore into the hearts and memories of all those willing to listen. Over the years, they've done their sacred work, often quietly during times when the practice of herbalism was unpopular or considered dangerous or even outlawed.

The plants are our elders as well. Here on this beautiful planet Earth, long before the human species arrived, these ancient beings endured, passing their seeds on, generation upon generation, teaching the interconnectedness of all forms of life.

These keepers of the green, both human and plant, have passed on to us one of the oldest traditions in the world—the inherent ability of plants to heal us and the planet. We honor their legacy and their amazing generosity and seek to pass it on.

Pause with me . . . take a long, deep in-breath and call in those special elders who have been your guides on your grassroots journey of healing and green wisdom.

Who are your most cherished elders, both human and plant?

I think of my grandmother, Mary Abelian Egitkhanoff, and of
Juliette de Baïracli Levy, Tasha Tudor, Norma Meyers, and
Adele Dawson and how they influenced an entire generation of
herbalists by their commitment and their passion for the plants.
Each of these elders was so deeply immersed in the green world,
acting as an emissary for the plants. What I remember most
about each of them is their ability to stay true to themselves,
to live their dreams no matter what, and to share what they knew
with others. —R. G.

Most people think too much.
Get them to laugh and
half their troubles and sickness
will go away, and
the blessed herbs
will do the rest.

—*Hortense Robinson (1928–2010),*
   Belizean elder, midwife, and herbalist

Stand at the brink
of the abyss of despair,
and when you see
you cannot bear it anymore,
draw back a little

*and have
a cup of tea.*
—*Elder Sophrony of Essex
(1896–1993),
ascetic Christian monk*

ECHINACEA

Echinacea angustifolia and *Echinacea purpurea*

If you only make one tincture for winter health, it should be whole plant echinacea. In late spring, gather fresh echinacea leaves, pack them loosely in a wide-mouth quart jar and cover with 80-proof (40 percent) alcohol (brandy, vodka, or gin). Keep on a warm kitchen shelf and shake daily. When buds begin to ripen on your echinacea plants in the garden, gather several and add them to the jar, along with more alcohol to cover. Later in the summer, add several mature flowers. In fall, dig up an echinacea root that's two to three years old, clean well, peel, chop into small pieces, and add to the jar. Let the tincture sit for three to four more weeks; then strain and use as needed for immunity support all winter long.

Don't forget to give thanks every time you harvest your plants and shake your tincture, to make it the best tincture you've ever had! —R. G.

how do plants give generously to you?

Old-growth cultures,
like old-growth forests,
have not been exterminated.
**The land holds
their memory
and the possibility
of regeneration.**
They are not only a matter
of ethnicity or history,
but of relationships born
out of reciprocity between
land and people.

— *Robin Wall Kimmerer*

Of all the creatures on Earth, the
plants have remained truest to their original instructions
from Creator.
They give generously of themselves
for the wellbeing of all.

—*Keewaydinoquay Pakawakuk Peschel*
(1919–1999),
Anishinaabeg medicine woman

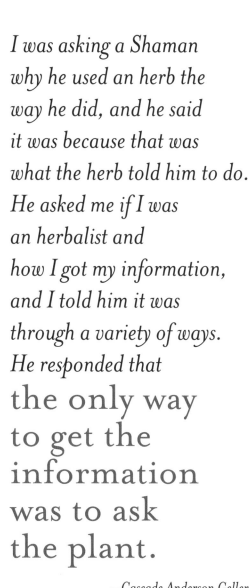

*I was asking a Shaman
why he used an herb the
way he did, and he said
it was because that was
what the herb told him to do.
He asked me if I was
an herbalist and
how I got my information,
and I told him it was
through a variety of ways.
He responded that*
the only way
to get the
information
was to ask
the plant.

—*Cascade Anderson Geller*
(1954–2013)

Just as the Elders of each generation are intent on
passing on their knowledge to all those
willing to listen and learn,
the Elder Mar tree shares abundantly with all creatures
who come to harvest her bounty.

ELDER
Sambucus nigra

This large, handsome shrub grows in many parts of the world including Europe and most of temperate North America. Wherever it is found, it has long been considered "nature's medicine chest." Elder flowers and berries are some of the best medicine and food we have and are easily found growing in the wild, especially along stream banks and in sunny fields and farmland. Not only are they good for us humans, the tender tips are beloved by deer, moose, and other grazing animals. Over 35 native birds are known to feast on the ripe berries in the summer. Plant it at the side of your garden, and watch the birds flock in.

When you harvest, always remember to leave enough behind for the wildlife. —R. G.

For those who live close to Nature,

each day dawns clean and beautiful,
and we can share it with our family and the
animals and birds, plants and trees,
which are all around us. Close to Nature!
The winds blow wild and the sun shines,
the rains come and snow comes also,
all wonderful things. We will refuse to let the
folly of others mar our lives completely.
Our neighbors may poison-spray their premises
and land, and the stench temporarily drowns
the scents of the opening lemon blossom
and the sun-warmed herbs in our own garden.
But the wind will come and cleanse
the air once more; always the wind comes.

—Juliette de Baïracli Levy (1912–2009)

The teachings are for all, not just for Indians. . . .
The white people never wanted to learn before.
Now they have a different understanding,
and they do want to learn. We are all children of God.

The tradition is open
to anyone who wants to learn.

But who really wants to learn?

—*Don José Matsuwa (1880–1990),*
Huichol elder

I'm going to share with you a prophecy of my own people, the Ojibwa . . .

They saw the comings of the Europeans to this continent . . . If these people came in a sacred manner and accepted the knowledge that was given to them by the people of this continent . . . we would walk as brothers and sisters on the land. Otherwise, prophecy said we would lie in the dust for 100 years or more as if we were dead . . . At the end of that time, we would be alive as if we were Earth Spirits just reborn . . . and we would return to the sacred path . . . The sons and daughters of the people who had come across the Great Water would come to us and say, "Teach us, for we are about to destroy the earth." This is the stage we are at right now.

—Sun Bear (1929–1992), Ojibwa/Métis sacred teacher

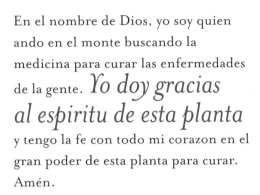

En el nombre de Dios, yo soy quien ando en el monte buscando la medicina para curar las enfermedades de la gente. *Yo doy gracias al espiritu de esta planta* y tengo la fe con todo mi corazon en el gran poder de esta planta para curar. Amén.

In the name of God, I am the one who walks in the fields searching for medicine to heal the people. I give thanks to the spirit of this plant *and I have faith with all my heart in its great power to heal. Amen.*

—Belizean plant gathering prayer, shared by Rosita Arvigo

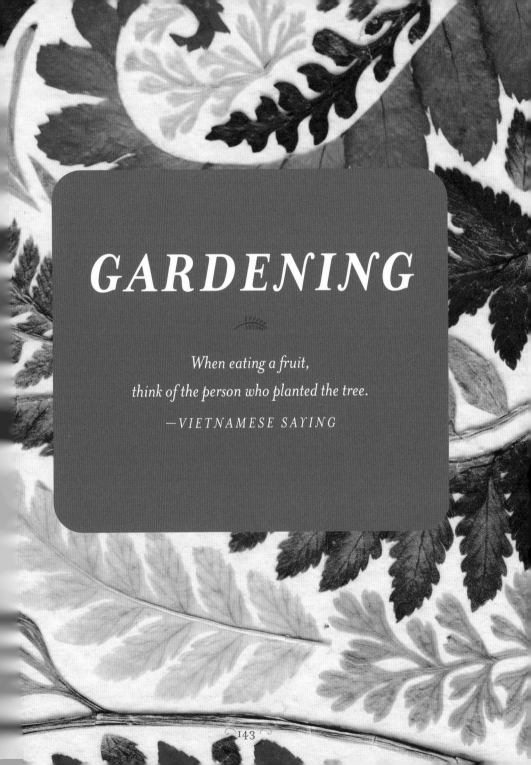

GARDENING

When eating a fruit,
think of the person who planted the tree.

—*VIETNAMESE SAYING*

Whether we're growing vegetables and fruits, herbs, or flowers (or all of them!), one of the greatest joys of gardening is the connection we make with nature.

As we tend our gardens, we observe the rhythms and cycles of the natural world, watching a tiny seed grow to maturity, flower, and perhaps seed again. This connection to nature and its cycles is integral to most traditional systems of healing.

As recently as one hundred years ago, almost every American household had a kitchen garden with an apothecary section where healing plants were grown. People made medicines and took care of their families from these backyard gardens and incorporated many of the tastier medicinal plants into their meals as well.

Tending a small herb garden renews our connection to the earth, provides medicine and food, and expands our knowledge of the healing plants. We also help preserve land by creating small botanical sanctuaries in our backyards, for every acre not built upon is an acre for the plants, pollinators, and other creatures. Habitat restoration and preservation can sound like huge tasks, but botanical sanctuaries can be created with any amount of land, including small backyards and front yards. All land is sacred, especially the land right under our feet. We just need to recognize and treat it as such. —R. G.

No matter how many years
I plant seeds and watch them grow
into full-grown plants,

I'm still overcome
by wonder and awe
whenever I see a
sprouting seed
poking out of the soil.

In a world growing more complicated
and technological by the day,
it's a comforting pleasure to
witness this simple, yet miraculous,
emergence of life.

—*Juliet Blankespoor*

The loving intent of creating a sacred and safe place

for native plants causes plants to respond with equal, if not more, loving vibrations. Within a sanctuary one experiences relaxation, peace, vitality, and an over-all sense of well-being. Here the common union between plants and people— breath—can be intentionally shared . . . In this open-heart space we move into harmony with the rhythm of Earth, taking our place in the vast web of life as a co-creative partner.

—Pam Montgomery

And don't think the
garden loses its ecstasy
in winter. It's quiet,
but the roots are down there,
riotous.

—*Rumi*

People often ask me
what one thing I would recommend
to restore the relationship
between land and people.
My answer is almost always,

"Plant a garden."

. . . Something essential happens in
a vegetable garden. It's a place
where if you can't say "I love you"
out loud, you can say it in seeds.
And the land will reciprocate, in beans.

—*Robin Wall Kimmerer*

ROSE
Rosaceae family

Rose, most ancient of flowers, has been revered through the ages for her beauty, scent, and sweet allure. Cultures around the world incorporate roses into recipes and remedies for joy and romance, as well as for sorrow and grief. Embraced as a flower that lifts the spirit and opens the gateway to the heart, roses are thought of as a symbol of love, fertility, and passion, and are used to lift and lighten the grieving heart.

As beautiful and giving as Rose is, she also has thorns that teach us to handle her with care. —R. G.

can you practice giving love and joy
like the rose, while also, like the thorns of the rose,
making your boundaries known?

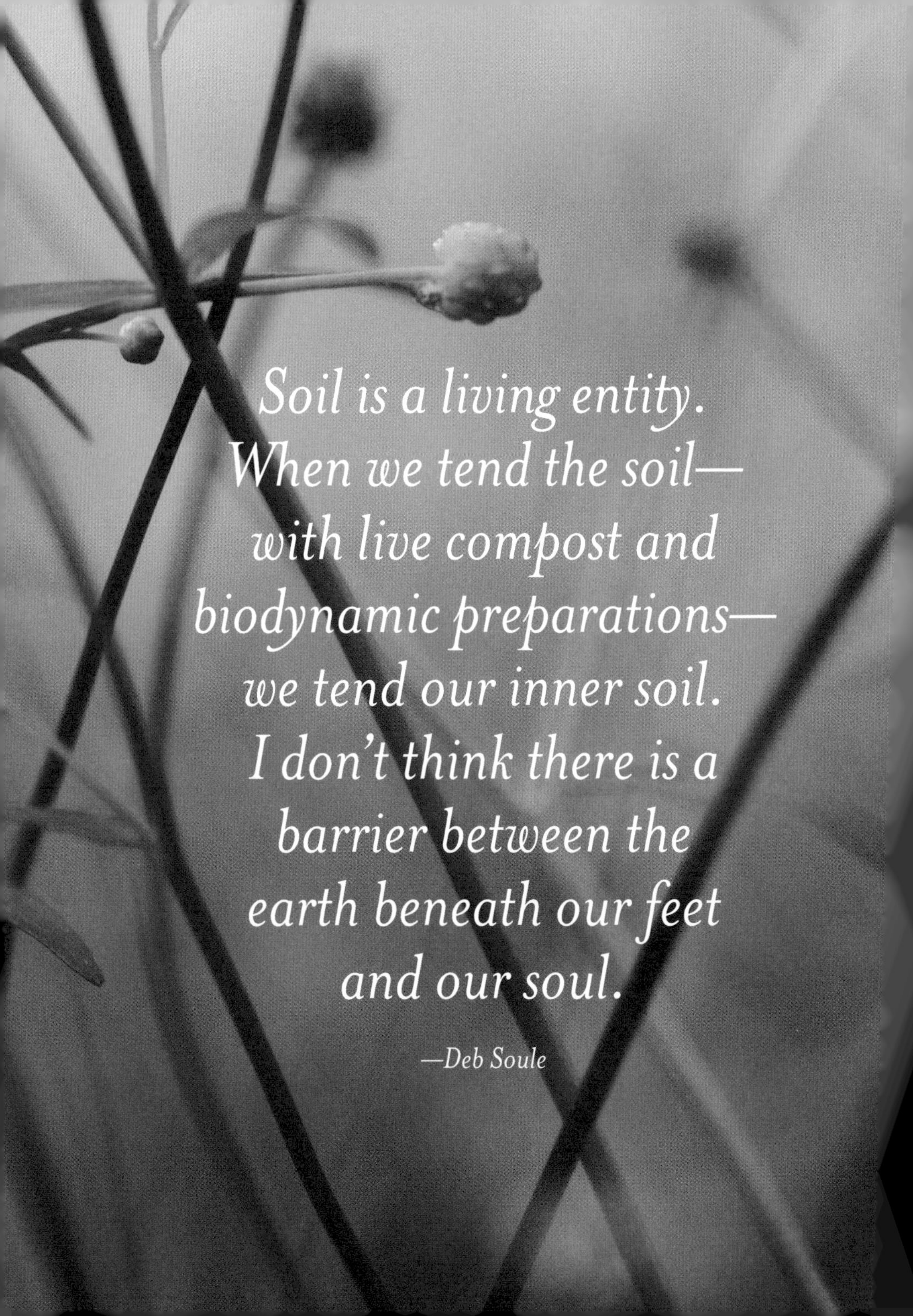

Soil is a living entity.
When we tend the soil—
with live compost and
biodynamic preparations—
we tend our inner soil.
I don't think there is a
barrier between the
earth beneath our feet
and our soul.

—Deb Soule

*Turn that worthless lawn
into a beautiful garden of food
whose seeds are stories sown,
whose foods are living origins.*

Grow a garden on the flat roof of your apartment building,
raise bees on the roof of your garage, grow onions in the
iris bed, plant fruit and nut trees that bear, don't plant
"ornamentals," and for God's sake don't complain about the
ripe fruit staining your carpet and your driveway;
rip out the carpet, trade food to someone who raises sheep
for wool, learn to weave carpets that can be washed, tear out
your driveway, plant the nine kinds of sacred berries of
your ancestors, raise chickens and feed them from your garden,
use your fruit in the grandest of ways, grow grapevines, make
dolmas, wine, invite your fascist neighbors over to feast, get to
know their ancestral grief that made them prefer a narrow mind,
start gardening together, turn both your griefs into food;
instead of converting them, convert their garage into a wine,
root, honey, and cheese cellar—who knows, peace might break
out, but if not you still have all that beautiful food to feed the
rest and the sense of humor the Holy gave you to know you're not
worthless because you can feed both the people and the
Holy with your two little able fists.

—*Martín Prechtel*

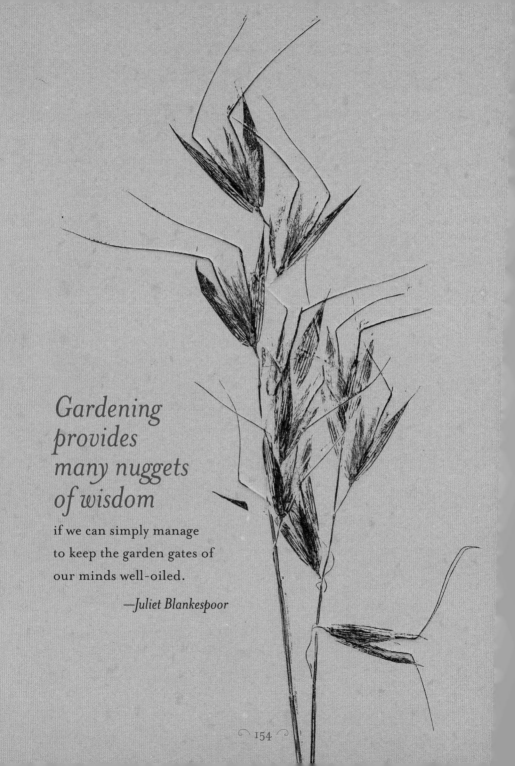

Gardening
provides
many nuggets
of wisdom

if we can simply manage
to keep the garden gates of
our minds well-oiled.

—*Juliet Blankespoor*

A garden is a
grand teacher.
It teaches patience
and careful watchfulness;
it teaches industry
and thrift;
above all it teaches
entire trust.

—*Gertrude Jekyll*

Gardens are such good metaphors for life.

I am always learning lessons.
Yesterday's was to be focused and
not let every plant live in one garden bed
so that it is so crowded
none of them are thriving!
Letting go of some things and
fertilizing the things that stay makes
for a more peaceful and
pleasant garden and life.

—*Nancy Phillips*

MY GARDEN FRIEND

I think the robin expected me.
His hops a playful welcome dance.
His head cocked, his inquisitive stare.
"Will she dig today?"
Sorry, my friend.
Not today.
I've set aside my to-dos.
Left my devices and worries inside.
Today I simply am.
Here, in the garden, with you.
No, no digging for me.
For now, I simply am.
I am here.
I am listening.
I am thankful for your song.

—*Rosalee de la Forêt*

*what new ways can you
introduce lavender into your life?*

158

LAVENDER

Lavandula angustifolia
and related species

What would the world be without lavender? It is first and foremost a beautiful, fragrant, hardy perennial that dresses up the landscape with its silvery gray leaves, lovely flower spikes, and fragrant aroma. Wherever lavender grows, bees and butterflies flock to it. As if its beauty weren't enough, this beloved herb also has a wide range of medicinal uses and rates high on the list of essential herbs to have on hand.

Lavender essential oil is considered first aid in a bottle; always keep a bottle close at hand. —R. G.

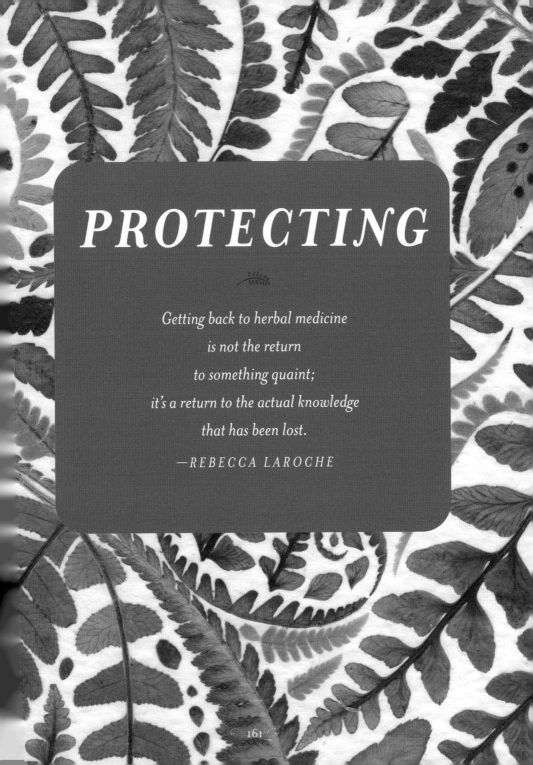

PROTECTING

Getting back to herbal medicine
is not the return
to something quaint;
it's a return to the actual knowledge
that has been lost.

—REBECCA LAROCHE

With the flourishing of herbal knowledge and the acceptance of plant medicine in recent decades, choices in health care have also grown.

Quality herbal products are readily available at farmers' markets, co-ops, and natural food stores. Access to herbalists, body therapists, aromatherapists, and other traditional healers has expanded in communities across the United States. Yet a surprise to many is that it is illegal to practice herbalism in this country. Offering herbal advice or herbal products for remedying a particular health issue could subject the practitioner to arrest. While some people believe that standardizing and legalizing herbal practice (and education) is the way forward, most herbalists and traditional healers advocate for a model that allows room for the diversity of ways that herbalism is practiced in the world today. Attempts to standardize the practice of plant medicine undermine the holistic nature and rich complexity that makes herbalism so effective. At the heart of this discussion is the right of every individual to have the freedom to make their own health care choices.

So how do we ensure that something that's been integral to people's healing path since the beginning of time is available to all without creating a rigid standard of practice? How do we protect health freedom rights while also ensuring safe and responsible practice? It's a complex and important discussion but the core goal must be to protect the right of individuals to make their own health choices, and to ensure access to a rich diversity of herbal and other healing practices. —R. G.

Unless we put medical freedom
into the Constitution,
the time will come when medicine
will organize into an underground dictatorship. . . .
To restrict the art of healing
to one class of men and
deny equal privileges to others
will constitute the Bastille of medical science.
All such laws are un-American
and despotic and have no place in a Republic.
*The Constitution
should make
special privilege for
Medical Freedom
as well as
Religious Freedom.*

—*Benjamin Rush*

Over the years living in the US, it has been my deep pleasure and honor to experience the vibrant, living tradition that is

the diversity of US herbalism.

To me it is *Viriditas* at work on a cultural level. This profoundly important phenomena (can't think of a better word this morning) should be cherished, not formalized or structured to death—as in Europe.

—*David Hoffmann*

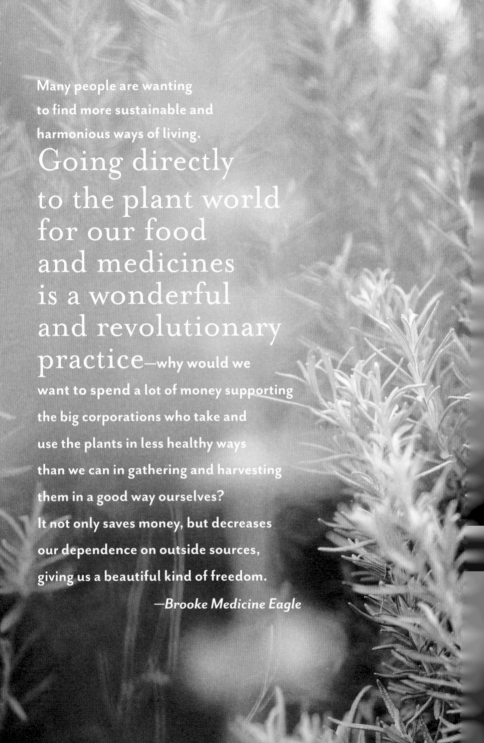

Many people are wanting
to find more sustainable and
harmonious ways of living.
Going directly
to the plant world
for our food
and medicines
is a wonderful
and revolutionary
practice—why would we
want to spend a lot of money supporting
the big corporations who take and
use the plants in less healthy ways
than we can in gathering and harvesting
them in a good way ourselves?
It not only saves money, but decreases
our dependence on outside sources,
giving us a beautiful kind of freedom.

—*Brooke Medicine Eagle*

*For two-thirds
of the people on earth,
traditional medicine
is herbal medicine.*

—Amanda McQuade Crawford

To make the acquaintance of an herb,
*to understand the
lowly weed, to hear
its voice and that of
Spirit teaching how to
make it medicine
and use it for healing,
is the essence of Earth
relationship and
Earth healing—the
essence of herbalism.*
It should be a simple thing
unencumbered by experts licensed
by the state. It belongs to the realm
where the human and sacred meet
in the plant. That is where it should
belong. As a result all healers will
find their own way and will always be
different. This is as it should be. We who
go before only point the direction.

—*Stephen Harrod Buhner*

Simple plant medicine
is more attuned
to the complexity of the body.

—Christopher Hobbs

Medicus curat,
natura sanat.

The physician treats,
nature heals.

—Hippocrates

YARROW

Achillea millefolium

Yarrow, you stand tall and strong, growing all the way from the sea to the mountain tops. You are a protective plant bringing strength and clarity. With a gentle rubbing of your leaves, your aroma delights and empowers. You lower our fevers and help us heal from the flu. You are always there to staunch bleeding inside and out. Wounds are no match for your healing powers.

Your stalks have ancient history in divining the I Ching.

There are many ornamental varieties of delightful color, but your wild white flowers and leaves offer the most potent medicine.

Stand strong and breathe deep.

—JANE BOTHWELL

Holistic cancer care is described
simply as collaborative care.
Nature is brought to the table.
Not as an alternative,
where it's all or nothing.
Not as integrative care, where
cultural traditions at the root of
natural medicine are diluted,
appropriated, and/or lost.
But rather as an equal member
of the healing team, with
the patient at the center.

*Holistic care is
expansive . . .
and inclusive.*

—Chanchal Cabrera

Ultimately, I was drawn
to herbal medicine because

it is a way of
saying there is
another definition
of what matters—

one that opposes isolation and separation,

one that acknowledges

that what we can know with our mind

isn't all there is to know.

—*Ann Armbrecht*

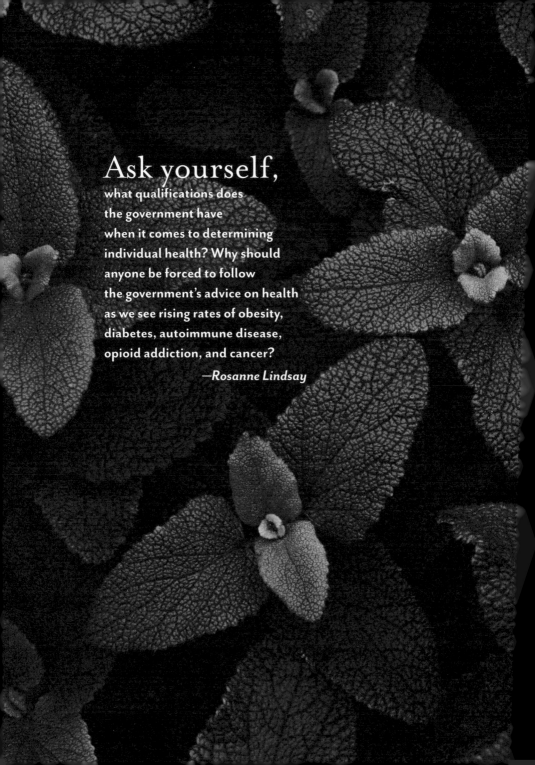

Ask yourself, what qualifications does the government have when it comes to determining individual health? Why should anyone be forced to follow the government's advice on health as we see rising rates of obesity, diabetes, autoimmune disease, opioid addiction, and cancer?

—Rosanne Lindsay

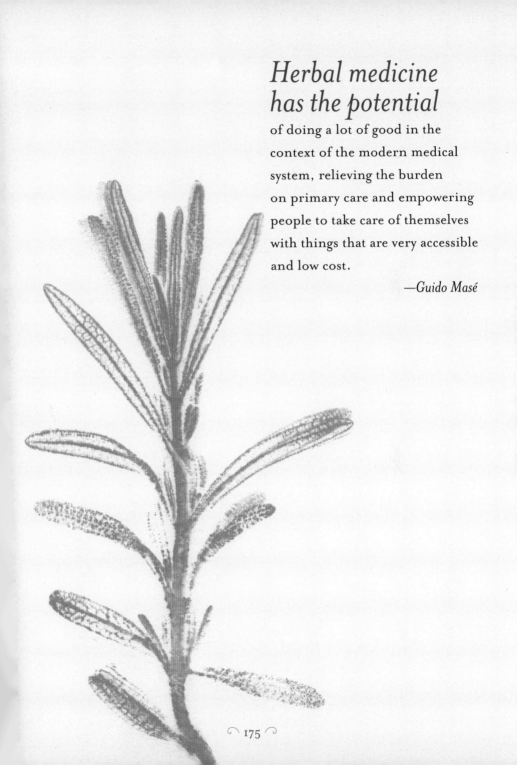

Herbal medicine has the potential of doing a lot of good in the context of the modern medical system, relieving the burden on primary care and empowering people to take care of themselves with things that are very accessible and low cost.

—*Guido Masé*

Prescribed, standardized coursework
will suck the flexibility and intuition
out of herbalism and create
passive students. Just like so many
other areas of expertise, herbalism
may become another field of cloned
book learners, instead of

a craft of unique,
plant-communicating
healers.

—Toni Manzi

There are no fixed methods
to apply to the
human predicament,
there is no single
all-pervasive rule to follow, since

*medicine is
not a science
but an art.*

—*Michael Moore*

The fuel which continues the fire or
life of man . . . is contained in two things,
food and medicines;
which are in harmony
with each other; grow in the
same field; to be used by the same
people. People who are capable of raising
and preparing their food, may as easily
learn to collect and prepare all their
medicines and administer them when needed.

—*Samuel Thomson*

For me,
the most
gentle
and least
invasive
treatment
that will solve the problem

is the one of choice.

—*Debbie Tuttle*

I am excited to see MDs becoming comfortable with herbs, but what really thrills me is seeing three-year-olds putting plants on boo-boos. *That is the revolution.*

—*Susun Weed*

Everything can be a poison,
and everything
can be a medicine—
it is all about context
and degree, relationship,
and dose.

—Bruce Parry

Herbs are not drugs.

Herbs work with the body's natural processes.

Drugs are often designed to force
the body out of the symptoms
that arise from our own innate wisdom.

—Christopher Hobbs

We are moving away from the idea that isolated, targeted chemicals—be they steroids, antibiotics, or other agents active at specific receptor sites in the human body—are the only way (or even the most efficient way) to achieve health-promoting effects. This is progress. But herbalism has more to offer to the field of medicine than simple polypharmacy: medicinal plants and their chemical cocktails don't just act on the system, the way a drug might, they interact with it. This means that, when taken habitually the way most herbal prescriptions are,

herbs enmesh themselves into our tissues

and processes, and their effects have as much to do with what the body does to the herbs as with what the herbs do to the body. Plant saponins are perhaps the best example of this, acting on every level from the formula to the internal organs and everything in between, changing their conformation and altering their behavior as they move through the physiology and interact with its denizens. If we can understand how a human being and a cocktail of botanical saponins relate to one another, then we don't just open a door to new formulation tricks and pharma-codynamic mechanisms—we get a visceral sense of how truly non-static herbal chemistry is, how it flows and changes, how different contexts affect it in different ways. And this may be the most important piece.

—*Guido Masé*

If the words "life, liberty
and the pursuit of happiness"
don't include the right to

*experiment with your
own consciousness,*

then the Declaration of
Independence isn't worth the
hemp it was written on.

—*Terence McKenna*

Herbalism
is the
gateway drug
to activism.

—Susan Leopold

Hot air rises,
so when
you stand up
for truth,
you feel the heat.

—*Cascade Anderson Geller*

ON BEING AN HERBALIST

*No matter our different backgrounds,
nationalities, race, or age, we speak a common language.
Our love of plants and the "green nations"
binds us together. Plants thrive in community,
and so do we.* —R. G.

I'm forever amazed at the varied and fascinating talents of my fellow herbalists. Many are not only outstanding herbal practitioners but also excellent writers, artists, musicians, farmers, and gardeners, as well as activists standing up and speaking out for any number of green causes. Plant lovers show a commitment to helping others along the green path and actively advocating for the health of Earth.

As we begin to study herbs, the essence of the plants infuses our life with greater joy and awareness. We become happier, healthier, more in balance, and in tune with our dreams. We quickly discover that plants offer far more than physical sustenance: in addition to food and medicine, they offer us a way of living harmoniously.

Plants constantly remind us that we are not isolated beings or single constituents with a single-minded agenda, but we are all related and are part of a greater community of diverse, creative beings. Plants thrive in community and the more diverse the community, the healthier the plants.

This is another lesson we learn from the plants: there is greater strength, beauty, and radiance to be found in a diverse wildflower garden than in a garden planted with a single species. –R. G.

The herbal village isn't so much a place or state of mind. It is in fact, a link connecting everyone around the world who believes the secrets to good health and a good life can be found in herbs, roots, and other "green" sources. *We all live in a single herbal village.*

—James A. Duke

When we succeed in looking at the world without seeing it simply as a playground for humans, we cannot help but notice the ubiquity of plants. ***They are everywhere and their adventures inevitably intertwine with ours.***

—*Stefano Mancuso*

CHAMOMILE

Anthemis nobilis and *Matricaria recutita*

Thousands of children have grown up listening to the tale of Peter Rabbit and his intense encounter in Mr. McGregor's garden, where Peter nearly lost his life over a stolen carrot. But Peter's mother, wise herbalist bunny that she was, calmed him down with a cup of chamomile tea. Chamomile is a wonderful herb to use to calm any anxious or nervous child (as well as their parents when their children go wandering!). —R. G.

Sometimes all it takes is a warm
cup of chamomile tea to make a miracle.
—Amanda McQuade Crawford

Reflecting on herbalism,

I can't really even imagine why everyone doesn't want to be an herbalist on some level. There is beauty and magic and adventure to be discovered everywhere on the herbal path . . . whether it's in our own gardens, on a woodland hike, or even finding a new and magical herb shop in a strange city. It makes me wonder what the world would be like if we were all just a little bit more plant-like and infused the world around us with beauty and healing and joy wherever we appear!

—*Emma Groff*

I often tell people that if we were to go into hard times, I would "kidnap" an herbalist, since I believe this knowledge is one of the most important things we can have to sustain our lives. I'm just kidding about kidnapping, yet I invite each of us to bring an herbalist into our lives and learn about the plant life around us, as well as support their important work.

Going direct to Mother Earth for our medicine and food is the healthiest practice we can have.

—*Brooke Medicine Eagle*

The poet's perspective of life, the musician's sense of harmony, the artist's eye of proportion and relationships—

these are all shared by healers, especially the herbal healer who works with plants, which are the pure creative expression of nature and the healing process.

—*Michael Tierra*

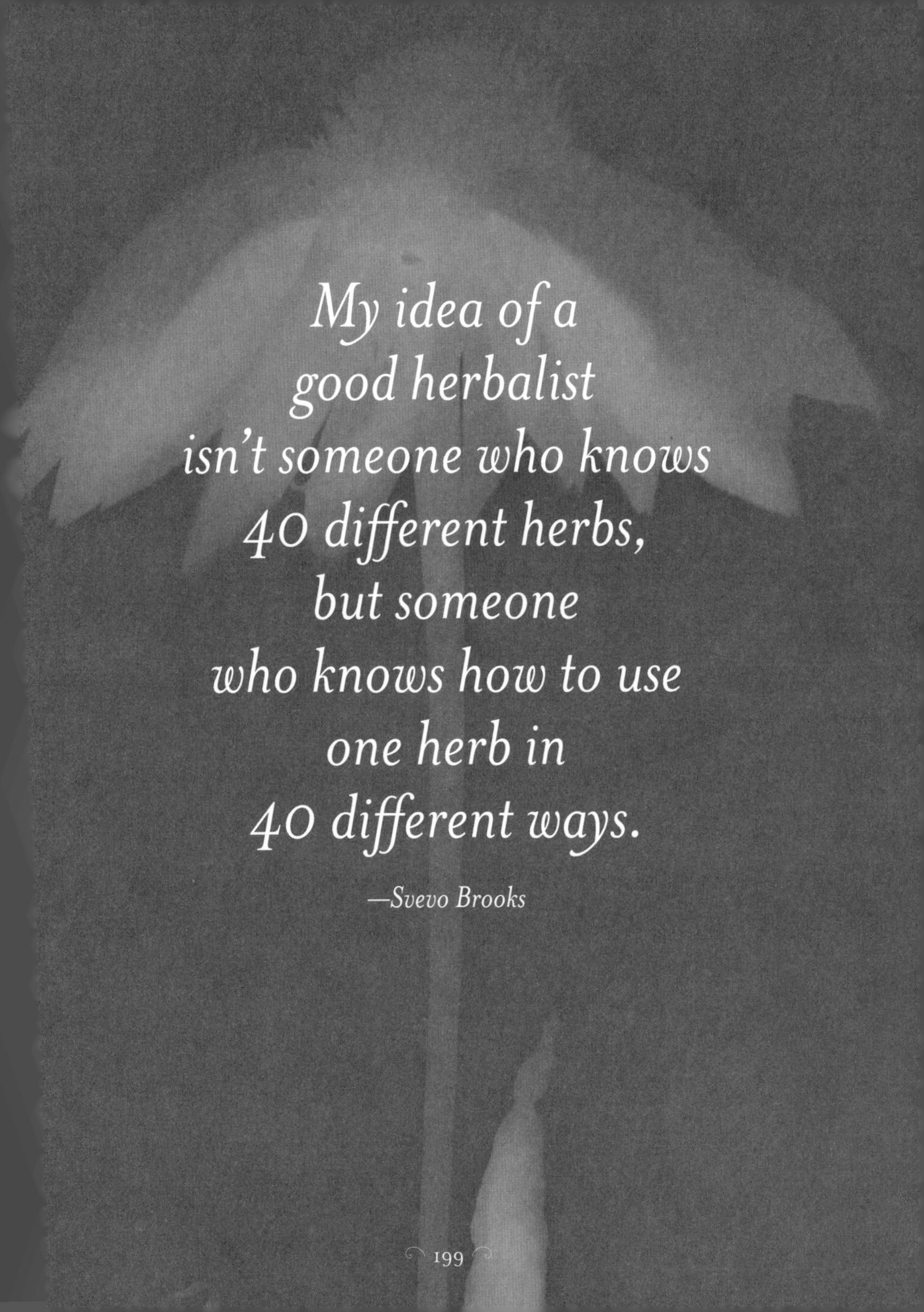

My idea of a
good herbalist
isn't someone who knows
40 different herbs,
but someone
who knows how to use
one herb in
40 different ways.

—*Svevo Brooks*

The human
being
is like a
garden,

and we, as herbalists,

are gardeners

working with a living,

intelligent ecology.

—*Guido Masé*

Becoming a person of the plants is not a learning process, it is a remembering process. Somewhere in our ancestral line, there was someone that lived deeply connected to the earth, the elements, the sun, moon, and stars. That ancestor lives inside our DNA, dormant, unexpressed, waiting to be remembered and brought back to life to show us the true nature of our indigenous soul.

—*Sajah Popham*

When you become a forager, herbalist, gardener, or plant enthusiast, you find yourself falling in love with the natural world over and over; you celebrate first blooms and new leaves, like the arrival of an old friend. And equally, you mourn the inevitable loss and cycles that nature embodies. . . . You begin to mark seasons by what is going to seed or fruit, and you may start to "feel" the plants before they appear. You bring gifts and offerings in your pockets when you visit to harvest the first dandelions, and it is not officially spring until you smell the first violet or eat your first bowl of nettle soup. You are attuned to the seasons, and plants begin to seek you out. It may be a subtle nudge at first, or like some kind of synchronistic magic.

—Tara Lanich-LaBrie

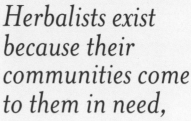

Herbalists exist because their communities come to them in need, herbalists exist because their communities support them. Herbalists learn more because their communities ask them questions and share their own experiences and wisdom. Herbalists exist as a part of an ecosystem made up not just— or even mostly—of plants, but of the connections between plants and place and people.

—*jim mcdonald*

MULLEIN
Verbascum thapsus

Sending stately flowering stalks several feet into the air, Mullein has a striking presence wherever it's found growing. In fact, it hardly looks like a "weed" but rather an exotic species that's been carefully tended in the landscape. Mullein will grow in just about any soil and in any condition. I've found it growing on the edge of woodlands, on railroad tracks, in lava beds, and on the meridian of busy freeways. It's a true survivor and thrivalist. But it also won't snub its nose at the comfort and luxury of a well-tended garden, and does marvelously when planted in well-drained, nutrient-rich soil in full sunlight, often becoming the centerpiece of the garden. —R. G.

For a truly colorful display,
plant Greek mullein (Verbascum olympicum)
in your garden.

*We are
healthcare practitioners first,
and herbalists second.*

—*7Song*

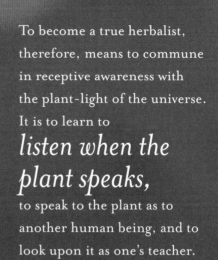

To become a true herbalist,
therefore, means to commune
in receptive awareness with
the plant-light of the universe.
It is to learn to
listen when the
plant speaks,
to speak to the plant as to
another human being, and to
look upon it as one's teacher.

—*David Frawley and Vasant Lad*

[Your grandfather] was always curious about other people's business, which is how he learned to be an herbalist. . . . As a boy, [he] sat in the hut of the herbalist in his village, ***watching and listening carefully*** while the other boys played, and in this way he gained knowledge.

—*Recounted to Barack Obama,* Dreams from My Father

They say we are engaged in
anthropomorphism.
My response: mechanomorphism is a
projection and it always has been.
We have a lot more
in common with a plant
than we do a car.

—Stephen Harrod Buhner

LEMON BALM

Melissa officinalis

Adele Dawson, a beloved herbalist who lived well into her 90s, grew copious amounts of lemon balm in her hillside gardens in Vermont. She made many popular potions—the most famous was her Lemon Balm Liqueur. When I would visit, often with a group of eager herb students, Adele would greet us at the door of her old farmhouse, holding aloft a tray of gleaming glasses filled with this liqueur.

Her recipe: Combine a handful of balm, a few borage leaves, 1 lemon and 1 orange (thinly sliced), 1 shot cognac, ½ cup honey, 1 bottle of claret, and 1 pint of seltzer water. Add ice to cool; strain and top with blue borage blossoms. —R. G.

What are the many ways
to enjoy lemon balm? Let us count them . . .

*I think healing
starts and ends with
loving each other*
and with caring for each other
as much as we care for ourselves.
It's the golden rule,
it's the way it works in medicine,
in politics, and in every aspect of life.
That would be my wish for people.
If I had no other words to say,
to love one another.

—Dr. William Mitchell

The secrets are in the plants.
To elicit them,
you have to love them.
—George Washington Carver

THE CIRCLE OF GENEROSITY

It is a great honor for me to be a gatherer and collector of these thoughtful reflections and musings shared by plant lovers from around the world. Many of these quotes were gathered from close friends and herbal allies as we spoke or taught at herbal conferences and events together; some were gathered from books they've written. Others were spoken or written by plant lovers from generations ago, but they strike as meaningful a chord today. Herbalists, it seems, are by nature a creative lot and have written and spoken endlessly and often quite eloquently about their passion for plants, so there is much to glean from.

Being a rather ardent collector of quotes, I have gathered hundreds (perhaps thousands) through the years, many of them equally as thoughtful and meaningful as the ones included in this book. But it would be impossible to fit them all in one volume. Winnowing them down was difficult, and I often had to ask for help in deciding what to include. My hope is that this collection of carefully curated plant musings will inspire and inform you to lean more deeply toward the plants, to listen more astutely to their often silent but still clearly heard voices, and to open your heart ever more widely to the many teachings plants have to offer.

In conclusion, I invite you to pause with me for a moment, together, to reflect on the generosity of plants and to give thanks for:

– The amazing abundance of food and variety of effective medicine that has kept us healthy and healed over millennia and generations

– The often beautiful and protective shelter that plants provide for humans and other animals all over Earth

- The luscious, sensuous fabric created from plants that protect our bodies from the elements—cotton, linen, rayon, silk, hemp, bamboo, jute, nettle, and flax

- The life-giving air we breathe

- And, perhaps most of all, the incredible beauty that plants shower us with. Everywhere we look, in every nook and cranny, hillside and meadow, desert or seaside, plants thrive, and where they thrive, they create communities of "beautility" (beauty and usefulness) as a byproduct of living.

While we create garbage dumps, nuclear waste, and harmful plastics that won't break down for millions of years, plants go about doing their work of creating healthy, healing, and beautiful living environments. Who are the wise ones, the elders, here? Without plants to paint our world a thousand hues, decorate it in an endless array of delectable tastes and textures, and scent it with an inconceivable variety of aromas, this would be a dull and lifeless planet. Who would want to live in such a place, even if they could?

What is our task in return for all this generosity? It's simply to love: to love the plants, love one another, and love this beautiful Earth Mother. What we love, we tend to respect, to stand up for, and are more willing to conserve and protect. That is perhaps our greatest task as plant lovers—to love, yes, but also conserve and protect this vastly huge and diverse carpet of plants that covers Earth, not only for future generations of plant lovers but, most importantly, for Earth herself.

May we all walk in Beauty and Balance on our Mother Earth.

—ROSEMARY GLADSTAR

FEATURED VOICES

7SONG directs the Northeast School of Botanical Medicine and is director of holistic medicine at the Ithaca Free Clinic, in Ithaca, New York. https://7song.com

MINNA THOMAS ANTRIM (1861–1950) was an American writer, well known for her collection of celebratory toasts, as well as books for children.

ANN ARMBRECHT, PhD, is an anthropologist, founder and director of the Sustainable Herbs Initiative, and author of *The Business of Botanicals*. https://annarmbrecht.com/about-me

ROSITA ARVIGO, doctor of naprapathy, is a world-renowned herbalist, founder of The Arvigo Techniques of Maya Abdominal Therapy, and co-author of *Rainforest Home Remedies*. https://rositaarvigo.com

SUN BEAR (1929–1992) was a teacher of Ojibwa descent and the author of eight books, including *The Medicine Wheel: Earth Astrology* (co-authored with Wabun Wind).

ROBIN ROSE BENNETT is a storyteller, writer, and herbalist who offers classes in WiseWoman Healing Ways and EarthSpirit Teachings. www.robinrosebennett.com

WENDELL BERRY is a poet, novelist, and environmentalist who has farmed in Kentucky for more than 40 years.

JULIET BLANKESPOOR is founder of the Chestnut School of Herbal Medicine and author of *The Healing Garden*. https://chestnutherbs.com

JOCELYN BORETA is an herbalist, community organizer, and co-founder and executive director of the Botanical Bus, a bilingual mobile herb clinic. https://thebotanicalbus.org

JANE BOTHWELL is a practicing herbalist and founder of Dandelion Herbal Center in Northern California.

SVEVO BROOKS, the author of *The Art of Good Living* and a former professional athlete and elementary school teacher, is a passionate advocate for outdoor public spaces.

STEPHEN HARROD BUHNER (1952–2022) was an herbalist and author of 25 books on nature, Indigenous cultures, the environment, and herbal medicine. www.stephenharrodbuhner.com

CHANCHAL CABRERA is a medical herbalist and author of *Holistic Cancer Care: An Herbal Approach to Preventing Cancer*. https://chanchalcabrera.com

GEORGE WASHINGTON CARVER (1864–1943) was an American agricultural scientist who promoted alternative crops to cotton and methods to prevent soil depletion.

LIA CHAVEZ is a renowned visual artist and the founder of Hildegaard, a creative endeavor dedicated to divine reverence for all of nature. www.liachavez.com

ELIOT COWAN (1946–2022) was a healer, teacher, and author of *Plant Spirit Medicine* and founder of Blue Deer Center. www.plantspiritmedicine.org

AMANDA McQUADE CRAWFORD is an herbalist, psychotherapist, and author of three books on women's health. She practices integrative health care in California. www.amandamcquadecrawford.com

ROSALEE DE LA FORÊT is an herbalist, teacher, education director at LearningHerbs.com, author of Alchemy of Herbs, and co-author of *Wild Remedies*. www.herbalremediesadvice.org

JAMES A. DUKE, PhD, (1929–2017), was an ethnobotanist and author of many herb books, including the best-selling *The Green Pharmacy*.

MARGI FLINT, a longtime clinical herbalist who lectures at herbal symposiums, medical institutions, and through Earthsong Herbals, is the author of *The Practicing Herbalist*. https://earthsongherbals.com

STEVEN FOSTER (1957–2022) was a botanical expert and renowned photographer who authored and contributed to hundreds of books and articles.

DAVID FRAWLEY, founder and director of the American Institute of Vedic Studies (www.vedanet .com), and **VASANT LAD**, Ayurvedic physician and founder of The Ayurvedic Institute (https://ayurveda .com), are co-authors of *The Yoga of Herbs*.

CASCADE ANDERSON GELLER (1954–2013), fittingly named after the Cascade mountains she loved, was an herbal teacher whose advocacy for the earth continues to inspire new generations of plant lovers.

JOHANN WOLFGANG von GOETHE
(1749–1832) is widely regarded as one of the
greatest writers in the German language.

JAMES GREEN is the author of *The Herbal
Medicine-Maker's Handbook* and *The Male Herbal*.

EMMA GROFF is an herbalist, yogi, mother,
beekeeper, and tech wizard for other herbalists.

THICH NHAT HANH (1926–2022) was a
Vietnamese Zen master, poet, teacher, and author of
many books including *The Miracle of Mindfulness*.

KIVA ROSE HARDIN is an herbalist, storyteller,
co-director of the Good Medicine Confluence,
co-editor of *Plant Healer Quarterly* magazine, and
author of *A Weedwife's Remedy*.
https://enchantersgreen.com

HILDEGARD OF BINGEN (1098–1179) was a
German Benedictine abbess, mystic, visionary,
and medical writer and practitioner during the
High Middle Ages.

JAMES HILLMAN (1926–2011) was the
founder of archetypal psychology and author of
The Soul's Code.

HIPPOCRATES (c. 460–370 BCE) was a
Greek physician and philosopher who is considered
the "Father of Modern Medicine."

CHRISTOPHER HOBBS, PhD, is a botanist,
herbal clinician, and mycologist, and the author
of many books including *Christopher Hobbs's
Medicinal Mushrooms: The Essential Guide*.
https://christopherhobbs.com

DAVID HOFFMANN is a clinical medical
herbalist, founding member and past president of
the American Herbalists Guild, and author of
The Holistic Herbal and *Therapeutic Herbalism*.

GERTRUDE JEKYLL (1843–1932) was a
horticulturalist, garden designer, writer, and artist.

KEETOOWAH was a wise elder and teacher
from the United Keetoowah Band of Cherokees.
He attended many of the early herbal conferences
and shared his wisdom generously.

JOSEPH KIEFER and **MARTIN KEMPLE**
are co-authors of *Digging Deeper: Integrating Youth
Gardens into Schools and Communities*.

ROBIN WALL KIMMERER is a scientist,
professor, and author of *The Serviceberry*, *Braiding
Sweetgrass*, and *Gathering Moss*. She is an enrolled
member of the Citizen Potawatomi Nation.
www.robinwallkimmerer.com

TARA LANICH-LaBRIE is a culinary herbalist
and author of the cookbook *Foraged & Grown*.
https://themedicinecircle.com

RAYLENE LANCASTER (1950–2012), also
known as Kumu Raylene Ha`alelea Kawaiae`a,
was a beloved teacher, practitioner, and preserver
of Hawaiian spiritual and cultural tradition.

REBECCA LAROCHE, PhD, is a professor of
English and the author of *Medical Authority and
Englishwomen's Herbal Texts, 1550–1650*.

DOUG LARSON, professor emeritus of biology
at the University of Guelph, studies ancient forests
and the effects of deforestation.

ALDO LEOPOLD (1887–1948) was a naturalist,
ecologist, writer, and author of *A Sand County
Almanac*.

SUSAN LEOPOLD, PhD, is an ethnobotanist
and executive director of United Plant Savers,
a nonprofit organization dedicated to protecting
native medicinal plants of North America and
their habitat.

JULIETTE de BAÏRACLI LEVY (1912–2009)
was a world-renowned herbalist, pioneer of
holistic animal health, and author of numerous
books on natural remedies and living in rhythm
with the natural world.

JILING LIN is a licensed acupuncturist, herbalist,
and integrative medical practitioner who teaches
Five Elements Lifestyle Medicine classes and retreats.
www.jilinglin.com

CHARIS LINDROOTH is a doctor of chiropractic,
herbalist, and founder of BotanicWise, a forum for
sharing plant wisdom. https://botanicwise.com

ROSANNE LINDSAY is a traditional
naturopath, herbalist, author, and president of
National Health Freedom Coalition.
www.natureofhealing.org

JOHN URI LLOYD (1849–1936) was an American
pharmacist and leader of the eclectic medicine
movement, which promoted botanical remedies.

SANDRA LORY, founder of Mandala Botanicals, an herbal sanctuary in Vermont, is an herbalist, gardener, and nurse who has worked on projects involving traditional and ancestral medicine, as well as food justice.

KAT MAIER, the founder and director of Sacred Plant Traditions, a center for herbal studies, is a clinical herbalist, teacher, and author of *Energetic Herbalism*. https://sacredplanttraditions.com

STEFANO MANCUSO is director of the International Laboratory of Plant Neurobiology in Florence, Italy, and author of numerous books including *Planting Our World* and *The Incredible Journey of Plants*.

TONI MANZI is a graduate of the Science and Art of Herbalism course and a practicing community herbalist.

GUIDO MASÉ is a clinical herbalist, herbal educator, teacher at the Vermont Center for Integrative Herbalism, chief herbalist at Urban Moonshine, and author of *The Wild Medicine Solution* and *DIY Bitters*.

DON JOSÉ MATSUWA (1880–1990) was a renowned shaman, ceremonial leader, and revered elder of the Huichol people.

jim mcdonald teaches classes and workshops with an energetic folk herbalism approach. https://herbcraft.org

ANNE McINTYRE is a medical herbalist and author of many books on herbal medicine and Ayurveda, including *Healing with Flowers* and *The Complete Herbal Tutor*. https://annemcintyre.com

TERENCE McKENNA (1946–2000) was an ethnobotanist and mystic who advocated the responsible use of naturally occurring psychedelic plants.

BROOKE MEDICINE EAGLE is an Earthkeeper, healer, and singer-songwriter who teaches at centers and gatherings across the US. www.medicineeagle.com

WILLIAM MITCHELL JR., ND (1947–2007), was a co-founder of Bastyr University, a practitioner of naturopathic medicine, and an author of books on naturopathic therapies and botanical medicines.

PAM MONTGOMERY is a teacher and Earth Elder, author of *Plant Spirit Healing* and *Partner Earth*, and head of the Partner Earth Education Center at Sweetwater Sanctuary in Vermont. www.wakeuptonature.com

MICHAEL MOORE (1941–2009) was the founder of the Southwest School of Botanical Medicine, an author, and beloved teacher of the bioregional approach to herbal medicine.

SIR THOMAS MORE (1478–1535) was an English lawyer, judge, social philosopher, and author of *Utopia*.

LUZ ELENA MOREY is a Columbian-born musician, teacher, performer, co-founder of the Vermont Wilderness School, and creator of the Gathering in Gratitude.

JOHN MUIR (1838–1914) was a naturalist, environmental philosopher and advocate, and co-founder of the Sierra Club.

JEAN NORDHAUS is a poet and the author of several poetry collections including *Innocence*.

BARACK OBAMA, the 44th president of the United States, published his memoir *Dreams from My Father* in 1995.

GEORGIA O'KEEFFE (1887–1986) was a modernist painter who gained international recognition for her paintings of natural forms, especially flowers and desert landscapes.

DON ELIJIO PANTI (1893–1996) was a Guatemala-born Mayan Belizean traditional herbalist and healer who used Mayan herbal medical techniques.

BRUCE PARRY is a documentary filmmaker, explorer, author, and Indigenous rights advocate. www.bruceparry.com

DALE PENDELL (1947–2018) was a poet, ethnobotanist, and novelist who explored the relationship between psychoactive plants and humans.

KEEWAYDINOQUAY PAKAWAKUK PESCHEL (1919–1999), an Anishinaabeg medicine woman, was a professor of ethnobotany and philosophy and author of numerous books on Native American medicine.

MICHAEL PHILLIPS (1957–2022) co-founded Heartsong Farm with his wife, Nancy, and authored *The Holistic Orchard*, *The Apple Grower*, and *Mycorrhizal Planet*.

NANCY PHILLIPS is an herbalist, holistic health coach, avid gardener, and co-author of *The Herbalist's Way* with her husband, Michael, with whom she founded Heartsong Farm in New Hampshire. https://heartsongfarmwellness.com

SAJAH POPHAM is co-founder of The School of Evolutionary Herbalism, Natura Sophia Spagyrics, and author of *Evolutionary Herbalism*. www.evolutionaryherbalism.com

MARTÍN PRECHTEL is an artist, writer, musician, storyteller, teacher, and healer. https://floweringmountain.com

WENDY READ is an herbalist, plant spirit healing practitioner, founder of The California Healing Institute, and author of *Cannabis Therapy*. www.caliheal.org

MISS HORTENSE ROBINSON (1928–2010) was a beloved and renowned herbal midwife in Belize and a fertility expert who taught at conferences worldwide.

CHRISTINA ROSSETTI (1830–1894) was an English poet noted for her works of fantasy, poems for children, and religious poetry.

EMILY RUFF is a community herbalist, the executive director of Sage Mountain Botanical Sanctuary, and the founder of the Florida School of Holistic Living and the Orlando Grief Care Project. https://sagemountain.com.

RUMI (1207–1273) was a thirteenth-century Persian poet and Sufi mystic.

BENJAMIN RUSH (1746–1813) was a Founding Father of the United States and a signatory to the Declaration of Independence.

BRANT SECUNDA is a shaman, healer, ceremonial leader in the Huichol Indian tradition of Mexico, and director of the Dance of the Deer Foundation Center for Shamanic studies. https://brantsecunda.com

CHIEF LEON SHENANDOAH (1915–1996) was an Onondaga spiritual and political leader, also known as Tadodaho, of the Haudenosaunee (Iroquois) Confederacy.

ZENKEI SHIBAYAMA (1894–1974) was Zen Master of Nanzen-ji Zen Monastery in Kyoto and the author of several books on Zen.

SUZANNE SIMARD, PhD, is a professor in the department of forest and conservation at the University of British Columbia and author of *Finding the Mother Tree: Discovering the Wisdom of the Forest*. https://suzannesimard.com

ELDER SOPHRONY OF ESSEX (1896–1993), also known as Sophrony the Athonite, was one of the most noted ascetic monks of the twentieth century.

DEB SOULE is an herbalist, biodynamic gardener, founder of Avena Botanicals Herbal Apothecary, and author of *Healing Herbs for Women* and *How to Move Like a Gardener*. www.debsoule.com

PAUL STAMETS is a renowned mycologist, teacher, medical researcher, entrepreneur, and author of six books, including *Mycelium Running* and *Growing Gourmet and Medicinal Mushrooms*. https://paulstamets.com

SAMUEL THOMSON (1769–1843) popularized herbal medicine in the US in the nineteenth century, founding an alternative system of medicine that became known as "Thomsonian Medicine."

MICHAEL TIERRA is a licensed acupuncturist and Oriental Medical Doctor, founder of the East West School of Herbology, and author of *The Way of Herbs* and *Planetary Herbology*.

TRISHUWA, a founding member of Foundation for Gaian Studies, teaches Earth-centered ceremony and spiritual practice. https://fgstudies.org/Trishuwa.html

DEBBIE TUTTLE is a Forest Therapy Guide and author of *Wealthy in the Woods: A Call to Deeper, Richer, and Healthier Living*.

SUSUN WEED is founder of the Wise Woman Center, a renowned herbal teacher, and author of five books, including *Healing Wise*, *New Menopausal Years: The Wise Woman Way*, and *Wise Woman Herbal for the Childbearing Year*. www.susunweed.com

REBECCA WESTEREN is a mixed-media artist and photographer, a graduate of the Science and Art of Herbalism course, and the author of *Handbook for Health*.

ZENSHIN, born in 574 CE, was the first woman to be ordained a Buddhist nun in Japan.

IN GRATITUDE

My gratitude for the herbs and the herbal community is immense. Once again, the generous and supportive nature of this plant-loving community shone through. Because if not for the generosity of this diverse community of plant lovers, which includes herbalists, healers, botanists and ethnobotanists, farmers, gardeners, poets and writers, and other plant lovers from all walks of life, this book simply wouldn't be. I'm also beyond grateful for all those whose quotes and plant musings I've collected over the span of years and wasn't able to use in this volume simply because of lack of space. Hopefully, there will be another volume . . . or someone will discover them when I'm long gone and decide to do an epilogue.

I, of course, need to acknowledge and thank my dear friend and publisher at Storey Publishing, Deborah Balmuth. Without her enthusiasm, hard work, and gentle guidance (a.k.a. prodding), all of these lovely quotes, plant musings, and reflections would have stayed in the dusty folders and files they've been stored in, many for decades. Deborah was my muse, my inspiration, and truly the co-author of this book celebrating the generosity of plants.

I also wish to thank the entire crew at Storey. They've helped make the creation of all my books less a chore and more a celebration. I especially appreciate the care and thoughtfulness they put into creating books that are not only informative and interesting, but look lovely, as well.

Carolyn Eckert did a phenomenal job designing this book, creating a look and finding the right images to capture the feeling of the words on each page. Endless gratitude to her and the generosity of all the artists who contributed.

And, of course, a huge thank-you to the plant families of the world for their tremendous generosity that inspired this book.

Writers often thank their husbands and families, because truly, the amount of time it takes to write a book is almost inconceivable and requires immense patience from family and friends of the author. Robert's patience has outlasted 13 books! We're still married, he's still patient, and patiently waiting for me to stop writing and have more time for him.

And, finally, I wish to thank the Garlic Queens, my sisters of the sacred clove, a close-knit group of aging herbalists, many whom I've known for more than 50 years, who have all lived quite spicy lives and have juicy stories to tell. I'm even thinking of writing my next book about this remarkable group of women herbalists and titling it *Chili Verde and the Garlic Queens: A Tale of Love, Friendship, and Herbs*. These women and their friendships have sustained me through hard times and good times, through unbearable loss and incredible joy, and they have danced with me on this herbalist path since the beginning of time.

GINKGO
Ginkgo biloba

Ginkgo, oh, Grandparent of trees,
you who thrived on this planet millions of years ago, and are now the
sole surviving member of an ancient genus of trees.

Called by scientists a living fossil, you hold the memories of a primordial
species encoded in your cellular memory.

When we drink your essence,
is it your memories entering us and the secrets of an immeasurable past,
or our own memory cells awakening?